Close Encounters

Close Encounters

100 Tips for Achieving the Intimacy You Desire

Marvin Stone, M.D.
Cari La Grange Murphy and Diane Stafford

Writer's Showcase
San Jose New York Lincoln Shanghai

Close Encounters
100 Tips for Achieving the Intimacy You Desire

Writer's Showcase
an imprint of iUniverse.com, Inc.

For information address:
iUniverse.com, Inc.
5220 S 16th, Ste. 200
Lincoln, NE 68512
www.iuniverse.com

ISBN: 0-595-17673-9

Printed in the United States of America

Contents

Preface

WHO WROTE THE BOOK OF LOVE?

Close. Snug. Spoonfitted bodies. Meshed hearts. Entwined fingers. Kindred souls. Getting close, closer, closest is something we all desire. Desperately. Problem is, most of us are better at sabotaging our efforts than we are at creating lasting bonds.

Intellectually, we understand the burning need for spiritual closeness—the desire to reveal secrets to someone who values us. We can imagine the joy of having a partner who understands our needs, desires, moods, thoughts—each day, waking up knowing that we share the most precious gift in life. No need to be vigilant because we trust our well-bonded unit, its two hearts beating as one.

Little wonder this sounds surreal. It is definitely not something that comes to us easily or naturally. Still, we seek it out. We want intimacy that evokes a loving sense of familiarity, attachment, companionship, devotion, and trust—an emotional safe haven that shelters during rough times with shared confidence, trust, and support.

So, what exactly *are* people looking for when they get married? "I wanted companionship, love, stability," says Lola Creeson, 28, who found those things with husband Ron. "I think your mate should be your best friend," says Carolyn Davidson, 40. "I wanted a gentle person who wants to understand your needs. Of course, most men don't understand them," she quips, "but it's nice if they want to..."

"Friend, lover, confidante" are three roles that Dave Waymond, 45, wants his fiancee to play. Basically, this tells us that most people start out knowing what they want—but are much less sure about the upkeep once they have the person socked away. What do you do when the inevitable yawns set in? How do you convince your spouse that you are his biggest fan? Clearly, keeping it real is a major challenge that requires compromise, effort, and mega-doses of love and passion.

And if you are genuinely fortunate—and can figure all how to do most of the right things—then maybe you will be lucky enough to arrive at that sublime state of quintessential intimacy that everyone wants—but finds elusive.

Question is: If it is, indeed, hugely important, why do so many of us falter—so often? It is simple, really. We are stuck with ourselves—and all the weird, quirky, inherent aspects of who we are. Toting the baggage of past relationships, we try to please—and make peace with—and enjoy fellow human beings.

But, the fabulous news is that you can actually scroll past your drawbacks and make your relationship a smashing success. All it takes is rethinking kneejerk reactions. Hold your partner's hand, erase and start over.

Here, we bring you 100 ways to heighten your intimacy. Sample a few, and we will wager that soon you will find your spouse smiling more, opening up, and choosing to spend more of his "discretionary" time with the person he likes best in the world—you!

SAYS WHO?

MARVIN STONE, M.D.

Dr. Marvin Stone is a 57-year-old doc-psychiatrist-who-solves-relationship-problems. Specializing in couples therapy, Stone spends his days dealing with couple trouble—but he is a big advocate of a here-and-now, pragmatic approach. "I don't want to talk about what happened to you when you were six," he says. "Some people are obsessed with what's wrong with them, but I always say, you need to cut the BS, find a solution, and let's do it!"

In his work with couples, he gets to the core of their problems in warp-speed time, in contrast to therapists who spend years doing the same thing. "I could make it take longer, but it's just boring, milking these couples for all they're worth," he says. "I'd rather be efficient in my helpfulness."

When it comes to medicine, Dr. Stone takes a holistic approach. "And I practice what I preach. I keep my body healthy." A marathoner and triathlete, Stone runs and works out regularly. He has a question-answer Website, and has written an advice column for *Texas Woman Magazine*. (http://www.intimaterelationships.com) In answering questions posed by the lovelorn, he likes to keep his responses brief, usually a paragraph or two, and people seem to relish his advice. "I'm able to help many people with their problems," he says. "And in sex therapy, 100 percent of them can benefit—*if* they listen."

He points out that one-third of the American population has sex problems that interfere with functioning. In the U.S., there are about 24 million people with orgasmic disorders and 15 million with desire disorders. In his daily work—and with this book—Dr. Stone plans to improve those statistics.

CARI LA GRANGE MURPHY

Cari La Grange Murphy, 31, is an accomplished writer, who has penned articles on love, relationships, and intimacy for *Texas Woman Magazine*. Cari has completed her second book, entitled YOUR SOUL IS CALLING YOU, and is currently working on her third book in the self-help field. Her writing incorporates a body/mind/spirit approach. She has a B.A. with a major in psychology. Cari's poetry has won several awards, and her poetry is posted on her Website. (Soulwrter@aol.com) Cari is certified in Reiki I and II and works to expand awareness in the fields of holistic health, spirituality, and physical fitness.

DIANE STAFFORD

Long-time writer Diane Stafford has been a key figure in a number of magazines, including *Houston Home & Garden* (editor-in-chief), *Houston Health & Fitness* and *Dallas Health & Fitness* (founder/editor-in-chief), *Latin Music Magazine* (senior editor), *Philanthropy in Texas* (editor), and *Texas Woman Magazine* (founder/editor-in-chief). A former speechwriter for the astronauts, Stafford now works as a freelance writer and edits books for Arte Publico Press.

Introduction

YOU, YOUR PARTNER & A FRESH SLATE

Achieving intimacy takes skills, and these are ones that few of us have. Developing this kind of expertise requires a strong dedication to making your partnership exceptional. You must be willing to nurture bonds of friendship and romance. You must give (and receive) respect, honesty, understanding, and ongoing displays of affection and concern. And, for the hardest challenge, you must learn to trust each other even though we live in a sex-obsessed society that mistakes passion for intimacy.

Although everyone who falls in love wants intimacy, many people give up without achieving it when they conclude—many times, incorrectly—that the "chemistry" is not right. Certainly, meaningful lovemaking is a great part of life, but without true intimacy, it is impossible to sustain passion.

Intimacy does not automatically evolve just because you are in love with someone. It takes time, patience, and focus. Both of you must be willing to share your vulnerabilities to develop high-caliber intimacy. You cannot worry about betrayal or loss of control. You must peel away protective barriers to discover the treasure.

Although the steps to intimacy are not mysterious and the skills are not complex, they are elusive, indeed. You must practice them, creating a dance in which neither of you leads but both are well-schooled in the choreography.

Close Encounters will help you recognize signposts, and by the time you turn the last page, you will anticipate the exciting adventure ahead. You and your partner—destined to be a truly intimate couple—will be set to share a lifetime of loving, warmth, and quintessential closeness. You want it. So, go out there and get it!

I

Emotion

1. *Why is a good sense of humor important in an intimate relationship?*

Smile. Sparkle. Laugh. Keep your heart light. It is extremely important to laugh together—in every room of the house. A good sense of humor will come in handy when you are dealing with your partner's imperfections and mistakes. Remind yourself daily that most of us take life too seriously, anyway. If you knew you had a year left to live, would you make a mountainous issue out of every annoying thing that happened?

Try a new approach; view your relationship as fun and funny. Grin at mistakes. Acknowledge flaws as reminders that you are married to a person, not a machine. (Chances are, your partner did not happen to stumble across the first perfect human, either!)

The power of a good sense of humor is that it turns negatives into positives. Laughter takes the edge off interactions by smoothing out rough edges. Without humor, life is more painful, and intimacy between two imperfect people seems virtually impossible.

To develop your sense of humor, laugh at yourself and let your partner in on the joke. Act silly. View problems like a child—with wonderment. To a kid, hurricanes and floods are larks. They get to wade in the water!

2. How can I keep from taking my partner's mood swings personally?

Like color chips in a kaleidoscope, moods are mysterious and ever-changing. And, they are part of everyone's life. TV sitcom moms may have been in a good mood for 30 years, but most of us simply do not feel perky every day of the week.

So, buck up and live with it. At times, your partner will get blue, and while it may have very little to do with you, it is still not a pretty thing to be around. All you need to know, though, is how to cope.

First, realize that most of us take moodiness personally when someone shuts us out. There is concern, and close behind comes anger.

If your spouse grows sullen and distant, you may feel ignored and irked. Worst-case scenarios come to mind, and you want some explanations. But what if your partner offers no explanations?

How should you react to mood swings? A key pointer is this: Do not draw conclusions or make assumptions. Never put your own spin on his silence. Instead, tell yourself that he is simply coping with stress. You cannot force him to open up. And it is not a good idea to act resentful.

Your partner's moods aren't expressions of feelings for you, so why look at them that way? Instead, show compassion. Give your partner room to think and come to grips with his emotions. He might decide to explain what he is feeling and why. Then again, he might not. And that is all right, too.

Just do not push. Once you achieve greater intimacy, he may choose to open up more readily. Meanwhile, stay supportive even when you find mood swings confusing and annoying. It is easy to make matters worse by drawing the wrong conclusions and getting moody yourself.

Bottom line: Mood swings are normal; you should not try to prevent them. Taking it personally will only make you miserable. Instead, go about your own life and stay positive. Keep an open mind. Your partner will appreciate your confident attitude and support.

Moods are real—and they are also inevitable. An inquisition that is not productive or necessary will only wither your partner.

3. How can we avoid the trap of being defensive?

Defensive? Not me! Truth is, *we all are*—from time to time. Some of us—most of the time. Basically, this is an area in which most human beings need improvement.

A defensive stance is no asset because it usually leads to anger and resentment, which are not exactly precursors of intimacy. If you continually attack and criticize, you are not taking responsibility for your own behavior, and, in turn, you make your partner feel threatened, insecure, and defensive. The push-pull of attacking and defending causes emotional and physical wear and tear. The answer? Learn to handle conflict with flexibility and maturity.

In an intimate relationship based on trust, partners should not feel threatened. You encourage communication that is open and honest. You try to understand and accept feelings and ideas that are different from your own.

Critical blaming forces you to defend when you should be problem-solving and working on communication. So, give these guidelines a shot:

Do not blame your partner. (Bite your tongue when you catch yourself.)

Instead of reacting defensively, stay calm and focus on the issue. Avoid "automatic defensiveness."

Do not take the bait or challenge. And do not accept responsibility readily. Be secure; it is fine to have your own opinions and beliefs.

Do not be offended by words, actions, or feelings your partner uses as weapons.

Never attack or push blame on your partner. Instead of overreacting when he says something in a way that sets you off, stay calm—and your partner will simmer down, too. This turns the situation into a chance to problem-solve. You do not have to find a scapegoat, and the argument does not have to escalate.

Remember that your partner does not have to share your opinions. You can be in love and accept each other's differences.

Use "I" statements instead of "you" comments. "I don't feel like you understand that I need privacy"–not "You never let me have any privacy!"

4. What is the best way to deal with possessiveness?

Forget the ownership thing; it is not going to happen. You absolutely do not own anyone—even though that individual loves you.

Possessiveness is destructive and totally incompatible with intimacy. You mistrust your partner, which makes you try to monitor and control his interactions with others.

Why do you behave in such a naughty and ridiculous way? It stems from your own feelings of inadequacy. You don't feel worthy of love, so you doubt your ability to hang on to him. In hopes of preventing your spouse from straying, you become possessive, vigilant, and watchful to the point of paranoia.

It will not be long before you are misinterpreting behavior and tossing out accusations. Your partner begins to feel hopeless because he is damned if he shows attention to anyone other than you—or if anyone pays attention to him.

Possessiveness is the sister emotion of jealousy, and both are relationship busters—destructive emotions that rupture bonds of trust and drive your partner away.

The answer? Focus on developing self-confidence, which will help you become more trusting, loving, and supportive. Faith in your partner's loyalty and dependability is critical to an intimate relationship.

Unless your partner gives you reason for concern, try to be optimistic and positive. It is your job to confront your own demons of insecurity and jealousy. Show your partner you trust him, and remember that people rarely want to leave someone who is affectionate, supportive, and confident.

Relationships are always a risk, but the more confidence you have and the more trust you invest in your love, the better chance you have. Trust breeds trust, and you cannot have true intimacy without it.

5. Are relationship ups and downs inevitable?

Hills and valleys. Seasons. Individuals and couples change and evolve, so you are bound to have periods of lust, passion, tenderness, sorrow, challenge, crisis, estrangement, companionship, and varying degrees of love. .

So if it is true that change can lead to transformation and growth, and that it does not have to wreak havoc, why do we freak? It is because difficult periods make us question our relationships: We wonder if bumpy spots along the road point to trouble in paradise.

Frankly, partners do grow at different rates, and when this happens, you will notice that you are moving in different orbits. One partner may have interests that the other does not enjoy. One person may mature faster in values, tastes, needs, psychological makeup, emotional stability. These disparities often make couples feel out of sync; instinctively, that leads to worries about whether the relationship is doomed.

What really matters? It is how you react to change. To stay intimate and healthy emotionally, you must grow together. You should complement each other's growth. Look at your ups and downs as opportunities to tighten your bond as you weather change and tribulation and come out on the other side.

If you recognize that all relationships have highs and lows, change will not throw you for a loop. And it just is not necessary to fathom every change. Often, the wisest solution is to stay out of your partner's way until the problem runs its course.

Down cycles always pass. Welcome these adjustment periods with a brave heart. Your goal is to strengthen the love you share. By standing united, you prove that the relationship can withstand difficulties.

6. How can I develop greater empathy for my partner's problems?

If you cannot walk a mile in your partner's shoes, you are going to have trouble establishing closeness. Empathy—experiencing feelings, thoughts, and attitudes of someone else—is vital to a successful relationship.

Ideally, you, as intimate partners, should understand each other's heart, mind, and soul. That kind of empathy helps you overcome conflict and leads you to make choices that are in the best interest of the partnership.

If you can fathom only your own feelings and opinions, you will not have meaningful communication. When you fail to empathize with your partner, it leads to conflict and growing apart. Ultimately, a lack of openness and flexibility leads to stagnation. To grow together, you must feel each other's joys, sorrow, pain, and excitement.

Of course, developing empathy takes time; you have to know your partner well. Talk about thoughts and feelings and attitudes—and listen. You might discover an inner self you never knew your partner had, which will excite you, adding vitality to the relationship.

When you listen and understand, your partner will know that you care and understand, and soon he'll feel comfortable disclosing more. No longer are you two acquaintances living under the same roof, but people who really know and like each other. One of life's best parts is being with someone who understands you.

7. How can we heighten our levels of tenderness and compassion?

Would you call yourself tender? Compassionate?

If you are warm, soft, gentle, and loving, cuddliness and closeness come naturally. You are sensitive to your partner's needs, and the atmosphere of warmth and gentleness nurtures honesty.

There is no doubt that tenderness and compassion promote sharing. Most of us feel like we can let our guard down in an atmosphere of love and trust, where feelings are acknowledged and not criticized. Unfortunately, some people are afraid to be tender and compassionate because they confuse expressions of feelings with weakness.

Partners need to be supportive during hard times and encourage the expression of emotions. Listen and offer a warm shoulder. Offer comments and express empathy only if your partner appears receptive. Otherwise, it is enough that you are close by and listening.

8. Why is the level of sentimentality dissimilar in men and women?

Hearts and flowers. Notes on the mirror. Some people overflow with expressions of affection. They are softies—sweet sentimentalists. We have all known and loved them, these touchy-feely sorts who toss bouquets of love, warmth, and tenderness.

But, the truth is, all of us are capable of sentimentality—even though most men are taught to be stoic and in control, while women are encouraged to be sweet and sentimental. This difference stems from women's roles as caretakers in our culture, which makes them more comfortable with emotions. Often, it is difficult for a woman to accept that her partner does not open up as effortlessly as she does.

The inability of partners to understand and accept differences in this area often leads to friction. Women hate that men fail to show their emotions, while men think that women go overboard.

The answer? Why not just accept that the guy in your life is not trying to be difficult, nor is he deliberately trying to make you unhappy? Men simply are not used to expressing feelings. Live with it. And on those occasions when your partner does open up, listen and enjoy.

9. How can I make my partner feel cherished?

Cherish is such a comfort word that songwriters pepper lyrics with it. Even the sound of "cherish" has a whoosh that reminds us of the blush of affection.

Great warmth comes from feeling treasured, adored, and appreciated. When you and your partner know that you are cherished, it is easy to share your deepest desires and fantasies. Conversely, partners who fail to make each other feel this way will never achieve the level of openness necessary for deep intimacy.

Unfortunately, after the initial stages of infatuation, we slack off on praise. In most relationships, all the compliments come in early months of courtship.

So, how can you do better than the masses? Simply take time to tell your partner how wonderful he is. And remember that it is absolutely impossible to praise too much. (Forget the idea of being overly effusive; this just cannot happen!)

Unfortunately, overkill in the praise department is not often a problem. On the contrary. If you are like most people, you are more likely to play up what is wrong with each other rather than what is right. But, why not try to be that rare and special couple who focus on the qualities that initially attracted you to each other?

This can be accomplished via strokes. Give your partner strokes day and night. When he does something that warrants praise, bowl him over with your enthusiasm. When it comes to showing appreciation, just keep it coming. Give thanks in every area, and that definitely includes appearance and sexuality.

Praise is one of the strongest glues in intimate bonding. When you accept your mate unconditionally, when you plant positive words in his mind, when you encourage him at all times, you make your partner feel worthwhile. When you accept individuality and give him the freedom to fail without fault, you build a connection that is everlasting. Why would he (or anyone else treated similarly) want to defect?

II

Communication

10. Can we argue without destroying intimacy?

In the final analysis, ask yourself what issues are really worth going to the mat over. Lifelong, we are told to choose our battles, but few of us remember this when we enter the ring with a feisty spouse.

While disagreements are inevitable, many of us have a terrible fear of conflict because we hate to see it escalate into a battle royal. This causes many couples to avoid the awesome task of resolving problems.

But let us rethink this matter. Tell yourself that conflict is not automatically a red flag, and it certainly does not have to mean that you and your partner are incompatible. Why not look at arguments as opportunities to gain insight into your partner—to know him better?

Of course, when you are close to someone, you are more likely to be strongly impacted by hostile behavior or angry words. But, the truth is, lovers can resolve differences without weakening the fabric of intimacy. Here are some practical tips:

- Avoid losing control of your emotions.
- Think before you speak or act.
- Focus on resolving the conflict in a win-win manner.

- Do not use words to hurt your partner's feelings or injure his pride. Damaging words will wound the spirit and weaken bonds of intimacy. You probably will not resolve the conflict, but you will certainly damage the relationship. (Imagine that your arguments are being viewed on television, or the Internet, and behave in a way that you could rerun everything that happened and not feel chagrin. Total respect. And no behaviors you would regret.)
- Instead of flying off the handle, gather your thoughts and plan your words.
- Be open and honest.
- Show genuine interest in your partner's point of view. Listen carefully. When your partner is speaking, make sure you are not formulating a comeback, which is one of the most common downfalls in communication.
- Stay calm, focused, compassionate. Remember that you are talking to your soulmate, someone you love and cherish. Use self-talk to remind yourself not to sabotage the relationship by saying cruel things that will scorch the heart of your beloved forever.

Learning to resolve conflict in a positive manner will strengthen your bond. A deep sense of caring and trust makes it less likely that you will fly out of control. End every conflict with a hug, which is a very powerful finale. Even if it feels contrived at first, try it; this really works. It serves as a reminder that you can love someone and not agree on everything—and that is really very much okay.

11. How can I motivate my partner to look his best without hurting his feelings?

So, you liked the way your spouse looked when you first met, but it has been downhill ever since... The guy has gained weight, lives in sweatpants, and has basically turned into a slob.

Where should you start? Show your partner how you yourself "clean up nice" and let him know this is important to you. Also, the days when your partner does look great, compliment him, hug him—be affectionate beyond belief. In other words, boggle his mind with positive feedback.

Never make fun of him or turn a cold shoulder when he does not look good. A slow "reshaping" process through gentle reminders works better, and gifts help, too. Be patient without being critical, and it is very likely that an improved version of your partner will magically evolve.

12. Can we turn conflict into an intimacy booster?

Frowns. Reprisals. Angry growls. It is inconceivable that anyone would think that any good could come of such dark components. But it can happen—by using loving tactics.

When you are at odds, work hard to maintain an attitude that is compassionate, open, understanding. Surefire deal-killers are hostility and demands. Listen and clarify issues as you try to understand your partner's needs. During the entire process of conflict resolution, reassure each other of your objectives and of your love. Also, try to keep close at hand a mental list of things you love about your spouse: "He's always ready to help me fix things." "She smiles a lot." "He's so sweet when he takes me in his arms to dance."

Remembering that you are deeply committed to the relationship will soften the discussion. (Remind yourself in the heat of an argument: "This man and I have a very good life together.") Successfully resolve each conflict this way, and your trust and admiration for each other will grow. Set your sights on an outcome that satisfies both of you. Take the idea of "winning" out of the whole thing.

13. When there is conflict and my partner withdraws, what should I do?

Does your spouse accuse you of bailing out? You have cross words, and suddenly, you throw up your hands and walk out of the room. Or you hang up the phone in his ear. This is called conflict avoidance—which can cause as many problems as bad fights.

Why do you bail? Maybe you wince at the thought of rejection, or you fear making your spouse mad. You may even assume that you will lose the skirmish, so why bother?

In truth, people who withdraw from conflict are actually increasing their chances of arguing in the future. Those big, bad resentments will not stay suppressed, and when frustrations hit a boiling point, uncontrollable anger bursts open. That is when all hope of calm problem-solving disappears.

We see a vicious, destructive cycle: Withdrawal frustrates one partner, and that leads to unproductive arguments, resulting in more conflict avoidance.

To get a handle on improving matters, try these ways of reducing anxiety during disagreements:

- Remember that avoidance of conflict is not a feasible solution.
- Approach conflict in a calm frame of mind. Stay in control.
- Use open, relaxed body language. Sit down and get comfortable. If you are standing, you run the risk of intimidating postures or hasty exits.
- Try breathing deeply, slowly, deliberately. Under stress, people tend to take shallow, rapid breaths, which only increases physical discomfort.
- Speak softly and slowly.
- Call a timeout if the discussion gets too uncomfortable or unproductive. A timeout is not withdrawal if you plan to resume the discussion after a break.
- Go at a pace that is comfortable and reduces the likelihood that either of you will walk away or withdraw.

- Remind yourself that effective problem-solving is a critical part of an intimate relationship. You do not have to master it, but you do need to develop some degree of finesse.

14. How can I promote open communication?

What could be better than sharing your life with a partner whom you really love to talk to—and who looks forward to sharing thoughts and ideas with you?

It all starts with loving, honest dialogue, in which both partners send messages that are aimed at increasing understanding, resolving differences, and creating an intimate partnership.

The three cardinal rules of good communication are listening, listening, and listening (everyone wants to be heard and understood). Only through listening can you come to know the person you love—his feelings, ideas, and needs. Unfortunately, many of us hear only our own voices and experience our own emotions and needs exclusively.

Most couples lack the skills of communicating successfully and managing conflict effectively. Why? You must learn to suspend judgment, validate feelings, discover the needs and feelings of others, stay courteous, and set limits. And even though this is a long laundry list, the truth is, you cannot have intimacy without good communication. Otherwise, you are just two people sharing living space while you wrongly assume that you are satisfying each other's needs.

People pretend to hear, but never fully listen, and thus, they never become intimate. You will only reveal yourself and risk being misunderstood if you feel very safe and secure in your partner's love.

Fortunately, communication skills are within the reach of most couples.

- First, give your partner your undivided attention when he talks to you. This means listening intently until he has finished and you have understood everything he has said. This will not happen if you're formulating your own response in your head while he is talking! Maintain eye contact to show your interest in what he is saying.

- Next, make it clear that you have listened by asking questions about what your partner said. Repeat in your own words what you think he is trying to convey to you. ("What I'm hearing you saying is that you think I'm too hasty in making decisions without your input...") Paraphrasing proves to your spouse that you were giving him complete attention and trying to understand where he was coming from.
- After summarizing, empathize with his message, and validate his feelings and needs. Use positive, assertive statements. Avoid aggressive or passive statements.
- Do not blame your partner. And avoid using negative statements.
- Stick to the topic, be courteous, negotiate solutions, and abandon the need to win or debate.
- When your partner knows you are listening, he will feel valued.
- Open communication allows couples to bond at deep levels. You will reveal more and more of yourself, and intimacy will blossom.

15. What can we do to keep bickering from interfering with our intimacy?

A bickering, squabbling couple is never a pretty picture. And it is one that we hate seeing—at a restaurant, on the street, at a party. The negativity bums us out. We vow that our relationship will never deteriorate to those depths. Not in a million years.

Usually, you cannot admit that you have fallen prey to this defective brand of communication. But what if you actually do nag your spouse continually about unresolved issues? If so, confront the matter calmly. Instead of nagging, take time to understand your partner's side of things. Stay calm, and so will your partner. Focus on a mutually satisfactory outcome.

To avoid the nagging syndrome, decide that you simply will refuse to let little things bug you. If your partner's way of problem-solving is random or disorganized, don't overreact. Help him to settle the little annoyances that come up in every relationship, but do not boast of your ability to do so.

16. How do we keep conflict on one issue—without rehashing old problems?

"When we were dating, you hung up on me and called me a bitch."

"Every time you do something nice for me, you always throw it up to me later."

"You flirted with that woman on the Internet last year—that counts, too!"

When you're having a spat, it is common practice to dredge up old and unrelated issues. Anyone backed into a corner tends to reach into his bag of insults and start slinging. When stressed and angry, you say things that are intended to hurt your partner. Later, you wish you had kept your mouth shut.

How can you keep this from happening? Try these techniques for staying focused:

- Agree on what the issue is and vow to discuss only that. If someone goes astray, call an immediate timeout. If minor side issues are directly related to the main issue, you can discuss these if they are ones you can resolve quickly.
- Stay calm, relaxed, in control. Avoid anger, which makes you say things that hinder resolution.
- Use active listening: Pay attention. Use good eye contact. Repeat back what has been said. Keep your pact to stay on target.

17. How important is mutual support?

You are his biggest fan. He acts as your number-one cheerleader. What a joy to know you have someone in your corner who is 100 percent on your side, no matter what!

If this is an area of your relationship that needs work, ask for the support you need. Express clearly what you would like for your partner to do.

Basic human psychology among caring, sensitive people shows time and again that we love to help others. But often, supportiveness may take a conscious effort on both parts, so do not assume that your partner knows what you need. Be direct; ask. If your partner seems reluctant to help, involve him without being critical. Once your partner sees how greater support cements your bond, it will become routine.

Unconditional love leads to intimacy. When you are supportive in good and bad times, when you acknowledge your partner's efforts, closeness deepens.

Having a partner who continually expresses respect and praise gives you confidence in your ability to pursue goals and confront tough issues. Conversely, if your partner takes your achievements for granted, you will feel estranged from him.

Everyone needs to feel supported. In any relationship, both partners make important contributions, and these should be recognized.

Be supportive of your partner's wildest dreams. Share ideas. Listen and be enthusiastic.

18. Is it possible that I am overdoing it when it comes to praising my partner?

Praise is ultra-cool. Kind and generous words can boost morale and erase the blues. In fact, the best way to nurture an intimate relationship is by expressing devotion and love through praise.

- Pay attention to your partner's moods and behavior, and praise genuinely from your heart.
- Notice things that you admire or find appealing and comment on them.
- Use specific details when expressing praise.
- Praise daily. It never grows old or stale. (But, guys, forget using the line "you always look good." It's not as reassuring as you think it is. Basically, it sounds like a disclaimer.)
- When your partner praises you, accept graciously. (Never say "I can't believe you like this awful dress!") Do not belittle words of praise. Your acceptance makes the giver feel good and promotes closeness.

19. Should we try to resolve conflicts quickly?

Got a beef? Then express what you have on your mind. And get over it!

People who turn disagreements into marathon discussions are doing little to endear themselves to their partners. In fact, long arguments are so tedious that most of us will do anything to steer clear of repeat performances.

To foster an intimate relationship, you must learn to resolve conflict as quickly as possible. Here is one good way to do it:

- Disagree in a supporting, loving manner.
- Listen without being judgmental or argumentative.
- Acknowledge your partner's concerns, feelings, and opinions.
- Use a nurturing manner of problem-solving.
- Do not fear intense expressions of emotions. If properly handled, these can lead to better understanding. With the resolution comes a renewed feeling of love.
- Avoid being defensive.
- Do not take the position of being totally right, because that makes your partner totally wrong. This bars the way to successful resolution

and leads to anger and resentment. Neither partner hears what the other has to say.

- Tell yourself and your partner that conflict is normal, and it can promote understanding, love, and intimacy. Couples who learn how to resolve conflict almost always wind up staying together.
- Give up the need to do it your way, and focus on what you can do to accept the opinion of your mate (while maintaining your own viewpoint). This turns conflict into a growing experience. Without quick dispute resolution, your intimacy will be ruined by resentment, bitterness, and hostility.
- Open your mind and heart to see your partner's point of view. Try to understand his feelings. That way, you can turn any negative situation into an opportunity for greater love.

20. How can we keep from misinterpreting feelings and intentions?

It is amazing how often tiny misunderstandings cause gigantic problems. You misinterpret your partner's intentions. Communication breaks down because one partner is reacting to an incomplete message or idea. A common response: "Why in the world would you think that?" "Where did you get that idea?"

To communicate successfully, you need complete facts. You have to understand the thoughts and actions your partner is trying to convey. Problems occur when you are unsure and you respond from uncertainty.

Everyone has patterns of speech and communication that are unique, learned behaviors. Often, you and your partner may have different perceptions of the same situation, contributing to defective communication because you do not understand fully what the other person really means.

You must be aware of the differences in how you and your partner view the world. Discuss your thoughts, feelings, and behaviors. Share your response to the issue at hand.

Making your partner aware of how you perceive an event or issue helps him understand you. Let your partner know your ideas, and ask him what else he needs to know to make sense of the situation from your perspective. Fill in the blanks for each other before jumping to conclusions. Take time to communicate clearly. Awareness of clarity is key to keeping things peaceful. Otherwise, misinterpretations can lead to damaging communication barriers and decreased trust and intimacy.

21. Why should we avoid the words "always" and "never" in our talks?

In the grand history of couple trouble, probably few things have caused more problems than the two innocent superlatives "always" and "never." They evoke anger and bitterness because they attach blame and make partners feel misunderstood and resentful. Examples: "We never go out anymore." "You never listen when I talk to you." "We always make love in the same way."

These words get a reaction, all right, but not the kind you want. Absolutes are rarely true representations, so why use them to inflame your partner?

The solution? Phrase your statements in more realistic language. Revise the above statements to: "We haven't gone out much lately." "Sometimes I feel like you don't listen to me." "Have you noticed that we usually make love in the same position?"

Change the discussion to an exercise in problem-solving, not sparring. Take a positive tact: "Let's go out more." "I'd like you to listen to what I have to say." "Let's try something different next time we make love." Simple changes in communication style can help you avoid conflict and achieve the results you want. Positivity breeds positivity.

22. *How important is it to express thanks?*

"Thanks for taking the garbage out!" If that sounds ridiculous, consider it one more time. Everyone likes to hear a partner express appreciation, even if it pertains to the most mundane household tasks. And why not? What are you out except a few seconds of your life and the effort it takes to say the words?

In relationships, it is easy to become complacent and ignore helpful acts and accomplishments. Partners fall into patterns, and good deeds go unnoticed.

Why not praise both ordinary and expected acts, as well as exceptional and unexpected? This is likely to please your partner, and he will be motivated to make you happy even more often.

Let your partner know how much you value him, and keep reminding him of your love. Never take anyone for granted. Thanking your partner is a simple way to make him feel especially cherished. Let him know you are thankful for each moment and each day of your relationship. (If you look at older couples, you will notice that a marked difference in their relationships. They show greater patience; most seniors simply do not want to waste time being angry or at odds. Time has become a precious commodity.)

23. *Can one partner's failure to listen hurt a relationship?*

Eyes glaze over. He stifles a yawn. Is he really listening to you? Or is this one more time when you are saying something that is important to you—and he seems like he is saying 'talk to my hand because my ears are not listening.'

Good listening means concentrating fully on what is being said. It is an important part of being a loving, caring partner, and most of us could stand to take our listening ability up a few notches. Here are tips for improving your intake skills:

- Pay close attention to your partner's words and movements.
- Make eye contact.
- Position your body in a way that shows that you are zeroing in on your partner.
- Offer responses that encourage him to go into greater detail.
- What if you see signs that your partner has no interest in understanding what you are saying? If he seems bored, impatient, or disinterested, it cuts off further discussion, and, as a result, you are not inclined to share what you have on your mind. As the ignored partner, you feel unimportant. Meanwhile, your inattentive partner is also bypassing an opportunity to gain insight into your thoughts. Obviously, some signs that your partner is not focusing on what you are saying are: poor eye contact; glancing around; easily distracted; zero feedback; interruptions

To be a good listener, you must be nonjudgmental and open to ideas and problem-solving input. Accept your partner as an equal, and show him that his opinions are valued and considered. Make eye contact, do not interrupt, and do acknowledge what is being said.

When your partner perceives that you are actively listening, he will know that you are taking him and his concerns seriously. This encourages sharing on a regular basis. Careful, disciplined, empathetic listening is a major contributor to intimacy.

24. Can we express anger constructively?

When you fail to try to resolve conflict through negotiation, understanding, and compromise, the issue does not simply go away. Instead, it festers and leads to resentment that pushes partners apart. Furthermore, when a couple fails to learn how to express feelings constructively, another downside is that sexual attraction diminishes. (It is clear in married couples that one of the main reasons for loss of sexual desire is unresolved anger.)

At the same time, you can both agree that, as a couple, you will have several "standing" issues that will recur. Typically, these do not go away; what changes is your ability to cope with them—and put them in perspective.

Here are ways to handle anger constructively.

• Express your feelings rather than hold them back.
• Be assertive. Speak clearly and in a straightforward manner.
• Avoid being critical, argumentative, or overly aggressive. Say how you feel, but do not attack or invite a counterattack or withdrawal.
• Be direct, calm, open, and honest.
• Express empathy with your partner's feelings.
• Foster a constructive dialogue.
• If you cannot control your anger, call a timeout to cool off. Leave the room for a moment. Resume the discussion when you can speak and think clearly and listen to what your partner has to say.
• If your partner reacts to your expression of anger with anger, stay calm.
• Do not let yourself be drawn into an argument.
• Allow your partner to express his anger while you remain calm.
• When he finishes venting his anger, proceed with an open dialogue in a calm manner.
• Use good listening skills and hope that your partner will respond in kind.
• After you both vent your anger, problem-solve through negotiation and compromise. The goal: a practical, workable solution.

25. Should I tell my partner that his mother is too critical and overbearing?

When you complain about an in-law, you're treading on sensitive territory. On the other hand, it is important to let your partner know how you feel so that resentments do not pile up, unaddressed.

Using a calm, nonconfrontational approach, point out the things that bother you, and ask for his help in addressing the problem. Tell him how her bossiness and criticism makes you feel, and brainstorm on ways to improve the situation.

Bite your tongue off when you feel like you are about to name-call. It is one of the most unproductive things you can do! And never make even the smallest insinuation that your partner is *a bad person*. Talk about behavior that bothers you—no more, no less. Discuss solutions.

26. How can I learn to be more assertive?

In any relationship, you need to be able to speak your mind, while still respecting the rights and feelings of someone else. Ask for what you need, state feelings, decline unwelcome requests, and resist exploitation. By being assertive, you are more in control of your destiny. People who fail to express feelings out of fear or reticence will grow resentful when their partners' desires prevail most of the time. By the same token, do not automatically assume that assertiveness calls for being difficult or resisting your partner's ideas. It simply means the freedom to speak out and thus, resist coercion and manipulation. Doublecheck why you are balking; is it just an old, familiar habit or are you taking an important stand?

Assertiveness also helps you set limits and establish priorities. Learn positive ways to speak to your partner: "I want...," "I'd like it if you...," "That feels good," and "Thank you..."

Negative assertiveness also has its place: "Please stop that," "I don't want," "I am not interested in," "That upsets me," and "I won't tolerate that."

Take a close look at this because you cannot be close unless both of you feel like you can freely express all types of feelings. To practice improving this area of your relationship, think of situations in which assertiveness would have worked better than what you actually did and rehearse what you should have said. Extend your assertiveness into day-to-day life inter-actions with people other than your spouse.

The more you practice assertive behavior, the stronger your self-esteem. Of course, assertiveness takes practice, but once you master it, the payoffs are greater confidence and intimacy.

27. In a good relationship, are apologies necessary?

When you whacked your siblings as a kid, your parents taught you the skill of saying "I'm sorry." Even then, it made sense, but as an adult, you may have grown more stubborn and thus, more reluctant to say these humble words. And that is unfortunate because being able to apologize is the lifeblood of close relationships. You made a mistake? So, why not admit it and move on. Remember, the person you are talking to is some-one you profess to love. Apologizing can help to stave off resentment, anger, and bitterness, and get your bond back on an even, peaceful keel.

In intimate relationships, you have the power to hurt each other deeply because partners are vulnerable because of trust, closeness, and intimate knowledge of one another. You know each other's weaknesses and sensitive areas.

To keep from injuring your partner, you must admit fault, which is not easy because it is always hard for people to express regret over something they have done. Most of us prefer placing blame.

The problem with being defensive and evasive is that these approaches keep an issue alive instead of starting the process that leads to closure.

Anything short of an apology and acceptance of responsibility damages your intimacy.

Saying you are sorry is a magic elixir. These simple words can keep you and your partner from indulging in hours of pointless bickering. Owning up to your mistakes makes your partner love you even more, and a ready apology fosters quick healing that leads to forgiveness and problem-solving. On the other hand, failure to accept responsibility spurs partners to dig in and hold on to positions that sabotage problem-solving.

Practice saying you are sorry. Ask for forgiveness, and accept responsibility for your actions.

28. Is my partner's silence always a bad sign?

Once again, he clams up. You face that cold shoulder all too often, and it gets old. You bristle. It is hard to view being shut out as anything but a personal affront. You wonder what could possibly be wrong with this dark creature you are married to.

But there is another course of action, and that is refusing to take your partner's silences to heart. Looking at periods of silence as negatives does not have to be a trap that you buy into.

You may be a person who expects a constant exchange of conversation, and when this fails to happen, you interpret the change as a sign of boredom or disinterest. But, you need to remember that people have different needs when it comes to talking. Some are content to do more thinking and just be in the company of a beloved. Others are uncomfortable with silence and need to chat continually. Neither style is right or wrong.

What is important is understanding your own style and that of your partner. That way, you will know the meaning of a silence . Obviously, when you're both angry or anxious, turning silent does not help matters.

But, it is equally disturbing to have your partner read a great deal into your silences. These are not always horrible signs, perhaps indicating that your partner has nothing to say to you or no longer loves you. Another possibility is that silence between partners who share a loving relationship merely signifies a high comfort level. Neither party feels a need to fill every void with chatter. On the other hand, if silences come from suppressed feelings or anger, these come under the freeze-out heading—a stumbling block that should be altered or dealt with quickly. When you have feelings that need to be resolved, fill your partner in on it; keep each other abreast of problems that require joint-venture handling. Maintain an ongoing open dialogue.

When partners know what is going on with each other, they can accept silences that are normal and healthy. At such times, simply feeling loved, understood, and secure is enough; no words are needed. The silence you share with your love represents trust, comfort, and security.

III

Individuality

29. Can a need for individual privacy interfere with intimacy as a couple?

You get upset when your partner sometimes locks you out of his life. He goes into his "cave" (computer room or TV space) and then you do not see his face for hours. Does this automatically mean there is a problem?

Not necessarily. Most people need personal space to know, enjoy, and love themselves; this is a lifelong enterprise. Periods of solitude can even replenish the loving energy that is necessary for intimacy.

Private times are healthy. You shift your focus back and forth from individual needs to couple tasks, and you do not need constant interaction for intimacy. In fact, a lack of personal time can be stressful because many of us use "aloneness" to regroup and wind down mentally and emotionally.

The key is balancing private time with couple time. Recharge your batteries, but do not let an excessive amount of solitude get in the way of relationship building. Couples need to share time, and individuals need to replenish separately.

If you feel satisfied, loved, and united, you and your partner have probably integrated needs in a balanced way. On the other hand, if you feel neglected and ignored, your mate has probably become withdrawn and distant, and change is needed to rebuild contentment and intimacy.

Private time should not result in deterioration of intimacy. Healthy relationships experience both oneness with and separation from a partner. Finding the correct balance allows individuals to appreciate themselves fully, as well as their mates and the time spent in loving interaction.

Take note of the amount of privacy your partner needs, and be respectful of this quirk. If you are overly cloying, you will end up smothering your spouse, and nothing good will come of that. Few of us seek to perpetuate claustrophobic situations. Just seeing you coming will make your partner look for an escape route.

30. How important are mutual goals? Where is this thing going?

Mutual goals are fun—and important. Short-term and long-term goals give you growth as a couple.

Your relationship should always move forward, with energy channeled into interests, education, financial stability, vocational development, family growth, and R&R. Stagnation spawns disconnected relationships.

Mutual goals help couples pool separate resources to meet challenges. You respect each other's contributions, and this brings you closer. When two people aspire to mutual hopes and dreams, they strengthen individual and shared potential for happiness. Successfully accomplishing team goals provides a sense of camaraderie.

Often, couples move in different directions. Because they are bound for different destinations in life, their intimacy weakens over time. A relationship is destined to suffer when couples lack commitment to the same goals and teamwork in achieving them. If your choices separate you from your partner, why not try to arrive at healthy and common decisions?

At the outset of your relationship, discuss goals. If your and your partner's are not compatible, it will take serious resolution for the relationship to succeed.

Find common ground in which to live and grow. Blending spiritually requires examining compatibility in temperament, energy, and commitment to the pursuit of aesthetics, knowledge, and love. You, as partners, have to turn obstacles into opportunities, dreams into realities.

As your relationship matures, update your goals jointly and celebrate accomplishments. Team victories build a spirit of togetherness. Mutual goals help you become a solid, goal-oriented team.

Of course, this does not mean that pairs have to share all their spare time. People can have virtually nothing in common when it comes to hobbies and sports, but still enjoy a very strong, loving relationship.

31. Is dependency a normal part of a relationship?

No one wants a clinging vine. A sycophant. A hanger-on.

The whole idea of having your spouse rely on you for sustenance is a turnoff. But, emotional dependency can also be healthy—when it means the trifecta of trust, reliance, and security. The key comes in finding a balance between needing and being needed.

Couples who fail to achieve the right balance are lopsided; one partner feels like a parent taking care of a child. Facing endless demands for attention and reassurance can make you feel exhausted and frustrated.

While it is true that emotional profiles are difficult to change, couples can adjust to each other's needs. Each partner must have a strong sense of self and bring vitality to the relationship. Combined, your strengths can make the partnership complete.

In intimate relationships, you are emotionally dependent on your mate to receive, acknowledge, and desire your love with a degree of intensity equal to that with which you offer it. Mutual dependence, which leads to security, is essential for true intimacy. Just be careful not to overdo it. Everyone wants to be needed, but few of us want to be a partner's entire world. That feels too much like a burden.

32. Do life's daily routines have to detract from intimacy?

Your routines should not cause conflict. These are simply natural parts of an intimate living arrangement. And routines can be used positively, as in scheduling times for romance—a vital part of a couple's regimen. Although it sounds canned, this is one way to ensure that busy people maintain intimacy. While spontaneous lovemaking is desirable, too, you probably need scheduled sex as well.

Giving time to the "couple thing" is every bit as important as nurturing your children. Do not fall into a habit of neglecting your relationship because your kids drain you dry. It is important to set boundaries that your children will learn to understand and respect; close your bedroom door; and take a firm stand on private time for adults, even though those self-centered little creatures you are raising can be formidable in their demands.

When setting up household routines with your partner, look for ways to share duties or do things in sync, though individually. Comfortable, predictable routines promote harmony.

Of the 168 hours in a week, figure out how many you devote to your relationship. If you say that intimacy is all-important to you, are you giving it time?

33. Will separate interests detract from our closeness?

Love me, love my puppy. But that is not always the way it works. You can be passionately in love with someone who sails, but your baggage is seasickness. That does not mean you cannot make it as a couple; it simply means you have an interest you cannot share. Often, having separate interests allows you to bring unique assets to the relationship that enhance your partnership. You develop your own interests and enjoy your partner's passions and accomplishments.

At the same time, be aware that too much separation can have a distancing effect. By the same token, do not get involved in your partner's interests to the detriment of your own (this can squelch your self-expression). Ideally, look for a few shared interests, and nurture some that are separate and all your own. You will always have the common denominators of eating together, living together, sleeping together.

34. What is the best way to deal with my partner's quirks?

She mumbles to herself while sitting at the computer. He talks during movies. She eats cookies in bed and leaves crumbs all over. He leaves the toilet seat up.

Quirks can get on your nerves, all right, but you need to accept and embrace the whole person you love. All of us have habits that our partners do not enjoy, but these things typically do not change in any significant way. Even if your love has some peculiar habits, changing him is not part of your job description.

Ever hear yourself say, "If only he would—." Or "He drives me crazy when he—." The reality? Your partner is a mix of parts of your own personality that you want and ones that you fear. Many traits you dislike the most are really ones you would love to have but can't. Accepting your partner, quirks and all, means accepting parts of yourself.

So, instead of trying to change your partner, take responsibility for yourself—only. Each individual perceives the world in a unique way, and each perception is valid. No one is "righter" than another.

When you fall in love and embark on a long-term relationship, take a good look at your partner's habits and decide if you can accept them. Once you move toward an intimate relationship, you must continue that acceptance. If your partner's behavior or habits drive you crazy, see if you can change your own perceptions. No one makes you feel or do anything. Why not choose to accept him as he is? Rethink it.

35. How can we inspire a sense of creativity and adventure in each other?

Stay playful. Grow. Explore. Learn new things about your lover.

Creativity can keep your relationship fresh, as sharing new experiences revitalizes your intimacy and love. Adventure and risk-taking are spark-plugs of excitement.

Relish in the playful side of your relationship. Encourage each other to grow and explore. Indulge in life's pleasures, and make sure that you do not allow yourselves to become prisoners of routines. To keep a relationship from stagnating, partners must investigate ideas, pursue new goals, explore unusual situations. Try new things and invite your partner to follow your lead.

How do you kick off creativity? Alter routines, for a start. Whatever you are doing now, look for ways to change. Be impulsive and silly. Take a one-day course in an offbeat subject. Go some place you have never been. Sign up for dance lessons. Try a new restaurant.

Either partner can take the initiative and let the other go along for the ride. Do projects together. Adventures will help to keep your relationship lively, and, in the process, intimacy will flourish.

36. What is the best way to deal with differences in education and economics?

You say "tomato." He says "toe-mah-to."

But, really, your differences do not have to be bummers. Most of us just turn them into obstacles. At the same time, you want to feel equal in a relationship. And even though partners often differ in what they bring to a relationship—in education and economics, for example, mutual respect must be intact. Condescending behavior has no place in a good relationship.

Be sure that you examine finances and educational differences prior to marriage. That is the perfect time to find out if you can negotiate these issues by giving proper weight to attributes like common sense, intuitive intelligence, and self-taught skills. Face differences, discuss them openly, and express concerns—and emphasize your partner's strong points—not deficiencies. Never attack differences; love is not about power or oneupmanship. Would you want to marry someone who is a duplicate of yourself?

37. How important are religious and cultural differences?

So, you have fallen madly in love with a Frenchman. He has only been in the United States for one year and seems steeped in the culture of his childhood. Two months into the courtship, he impetuously puts an engagement ring on your finger and insists you move in with him. It feels wildly romantic, being swept off your feet, but no sooner are you in the door than Froggie starts dictating how you both will live. Where is the partnership concept you grew up expecting? You say that since you both work long hours, you want to dine out three nights a week. He says he will cook every night, and you will eat out once a month—end of discussion.

Yes, different cultures can cause problems. Some people expect a very traditional approach to marriage, while others want to forge their own new path. You must find a way to negotiate religious and cultural issues because these things affect values, child-rearing, customs, spiritual beliefs, sexuality, intimacy, and social interactions.

Study religious and cultural differences carefully prior to marriage. If tensions crop up, you must use compromise to achieve harmony. Because you are dealing with emotionally charged issues, the aid of a mediator or counselor can be helpful.

Assess what needs to be discussed. Decide how you can blend your backgrounds—and how you are going to deal with differences in your extended families. Face questions head on.

Compromising on differences in religion and culture requires trust, aggressive dialogue, and commitment. Although rarely discussed prior to marriage, the spiritual component of a relationship is important. Finding a workable plan can provide the backbone of strong spiritual love.

38. Is it realistic to expect my partner to make changes to please me?

He would be perfect if he had a better job...or more hair...or took off twenty pounds. Many people obsess about changes that would make their partner "just right."

If you find yourself focusing on negative traits, or imagining how great he would be if only he made certain changes, face the fact that your premise for the relationship is flawed. The reason is simple; a good relationship is based on unconditional love, not rehauls. You love the person he is, not how he would be after he made a few much-needed changes. And you are definitely asking for trouble if you demand change or if you are preoccupied with your partner's shortcomings.

The irony is that during courtship, people often overlook traits they dislike, but later, the same characteristics become bones of contention when the blush of new love has faded. Example: Your guy smokes three packs a day and you are an anti-tobacco militant…but, wow, he is so darn cute and has those great blue eyes and that killer body . The first-month infatuation syndrome changes dramatically three months later when you begin to take off the blinders and think about a lifetime of second-hand smoke.

Demanding your partner make changes is not fair or healthy because it is not your job to shape him up. He does not want you to be his shrink, his personal trainer, or his diet consultant. Your premise should be that both of you are lovable just the way you are; genuine intimacy depends on unconditional acceptance. If you cannot give it, you need to spend some more time in self-examination.

Acceptance does not mean that you have to love every atom of your partner's being, everything he says, every move he makes—but you cannot obsess about change. You have to assume that you are marrying an individual who has his own set of existing positives and negatives (no improvements guaranteed). If he gets smart and stops smoking, that will be gravy, but you cannot make it your job to be his health policeman.

In looking at a potential partner, you absolutely must focus on the positive attributes that made you love him in the first place—and decide if that will carry you through decades of this partnership harmoniously.

39. What is the best way to deal with my partner's roving eye?

You sit in a restaurant with your guy, and he frequently glances at women who walk by. It bothers you, but you have no idea whether this would be a problem in marriage someday.

Well, a roving eye unnerves many of us. People who continually stare at attractive members of the opposite sex often make their partners uncomfortable. You do not want to make a partner feel like he is under surveillance, but, at the same time, it seems like there should be an answer. And there is. You can cope by doing your own share of admiring the opposite sex. If that does not interest you, you can always take the stand that you do not mind his wistful glances as long as roving-eye-boy is truly yours at day's end.

The most typical response, of course, is a wholehearted negative reaction. The kneejerk tendency is a quick assumption that you no longer appeal to your mate, and that explains why he would be shopping around.

If your partner ogles others, tackle the problem by trying to figure out what it means. How do you feel about it? What does the behavior mean to you and your partner? Should you tolerate it? If you have a strong self-image—and you decide the behavior is tolerable, you may be able to ignore it. After all, it is not really abnormal to stare at attractive members of the opposite sex; in fact, it is healthy to notice attractive people. But you should ask yourself these questions: Does he stare intensely? Does he look at other women in inappropriate situations? Is he unfazed by the fact that his behavior bothers you?

By all means, let your partner know he is making you uncomfortable. His number-one concern should be your feelings. It is a mistake on one partner's part to continue any behavior that makes the other party feel like he is not showing respect, attention, and love.

40. Will casual flirtations hurt our relationship?

Your darling has a tendency to flirt. In fact, he is widely known as a big flirt. A rogue. A player. Unfortunately, this reputation of his makes you feel insecure.

There is no one right or wrong way to handle this kind of behavior. But the issue of respect and love is very critical. It is entirely possible that your partner may be able to flirt and still manage to make you feel loved and respected. In such cases, flirting can be fun, irrelevant, and at times even a turn-on. Some people actually like to watch their partner flirt; for them, the fact that their mate appeals to others is an erotic stimulant.

On the other hand, even though flirting usually is not a sure sign of defection, you may be the kind of person who finds it devastating. If so, your partner must face the fact that his behavior is detrimental to a good relationship with you. You must convey to him that his flirting makes you feel like he has lost interest in you, or that it embarrasses you. At any rate, discuss the matter until you reach a solution that is suitable for both of you. Flirting is more aggressive than mere staring, and that means it is a form of behavior that should be looked at more carefully.

41. Is it healthy to express expectations?

You date a smart guy who is clearly failing to live up to his potential. You can imagine him really going places, being someone, making lots of money... But is it all right to expect your positive expectations to motivate him?

This is a touchy subject. It is always a good idea to encourage your partner. But it is unhealthy to set up goals for someone else, especially if these are unrealistic. Very quickly, your expectations will frustrate your partner and hurt your relationship.

It is perfectly all right to have expectations for yourself; you can handle those because you can control your own mind. But setting goals for a partner is problematic; remember, you are not in a relationship to "fix" someone.

Your partner is not supposed to give meaning to your life. View him in a realistic light that is free of unfair standards. Be tolerant and accepting.

IV

Sex

42. Does infrequent sex mean our relationship is in trouble?

You have been married for less than a year, but your husband is already making excuses to avoid having sex: He had a rough day. His workout wore him out. He has a headache.

Many people view changing sex patterns as a red flag. But the truth is, such complaints are common. Inconsistent and unsatisfactory sex plagues many couples. As time goes by, sex becomes a lower priority. You may feel less aroused, and your desire may be lower than it once was.

Many couples go through periods of sexual dissatisfaction. Frequency of lovemaking varies widely. Then, as you age, you face adjustments.

Problems sometimes stem from bouts of poor body image, which can lead to a deterioration in sexual satisfaction (you avoid lovemaking because you doubt that your body is still appealing). The birth of children often results in problems, from reduced privacy to a woman's fixation on her maternal role (she has trouble switching from mother to lover). In many cases, women redefine themselves as mothers exclusively after they have children, and this leaves their husbands out in the cold. Not only has he lost his wife's time and attentions, she is so comfortable with her newly altered role that he is left wondering what went wrong—and why he feels so alone and unhappy. He married a wife, but she shrugged that off as soon as the baby came in the door.

Anger, anxiety, resentment, and disappointment all work against good sex. When negative baggage accumulates, it affects coupling, no doubt about it. That is why it is important for couples to deal with these issues in a candid, honest manner; settling for unsatisfactory sex is flat-out silly.

You should admit, as partners, that many factors are going to eat up time and deplete energy. But instead of accepting a sex life that is not satisfying to you, focus on your relationship and talk about the reasons sex has become less frequent. Most importantly, find ways to get things back to the way you like them.

Avoid the pitfalls of predictability and boredom by taking the time to enhance your sensuality and seductiveness. Ignore stereotypes; you can make up your own mind about what constitutes a sexy body and a good lover.

Three guidelines can help you keep your sex life a strong element of your relationship: (1) Make your mate feel sexy and valued as a wonderful lover. Tell him about it. (2) Resolve resentments so that anger will not distance you from your partner. Making love includes body, mind, and spirit. If you let hostility creep in, sex will become a distant memory. (3) Set priorities to combat enemies of closeness like fatigue, stress, and busy schedules. For loving partners, the right setting will almost always give rise to sexual play.

As true companions over the years, you will develop a sexual comfort level. Sex is not the most important part of a marriage, nor does great sex ensure a great marriage. But a loving companionship is the foundation for intimate lovemaking. Strive to increase intimacy first, and passionate, satisfying sex will follow. Clear your mind, and concentrate on making your partner feel wonderful.

43. What can we do to spice up our sex lives?

Dog collars and chains? A little whipped cream? Maybe you are not into kinky stuff—and that is quite all right. What is not okay is failing to look for new ways to stimulate eroticism. That does not mean abandoning tried-and-true sexual activities that work. It just means making changes to reenergize.

Think creatively. Spice things up on your own or collaborate with your partner. You can kick off the process by telling your partner—share what you think you would like to try.

Simple adjustments can heighten romance to an amazing degree: Go to Erotic Boutique and buy a tiny lace teddy or hot-looking thong to surprise him. Suggest a new time of day or place for sex. Use soft lights, music, and candles. Give your partner an erotic massage, exploring his body and discovering new ways to turn him. Fondle with feathers, tongue, fingers, lips. Try new twists, limited only by your comfort levels.

Want something surefire? Create a dimly lit romantic setting with candles and erotic fragrances. Talk about how wonderful it will feel to touch and enjoy each other. Start massaging and slowly build the level of erotic touch. Allow your mind to delve deeply into erotic fantasies. Once you are both aroused, use a new technique to bring your partner to orgasm, or sample a new position. Get out of your comfort zone.

Sex is erotic play, and it is a great way to lose yourself completely in sensual feelings. Remember that your own bed is one place where it is quite all right to lose control.

44. Is it a good idea to discuss our past sex lives?

So, how many guys have you been to bed with? And who was your best lover—and why? Your partner may ask such questions—but if you are smart, you will not believe for one minute that he can actually handle the answers. Yes, he wants to know. No, he will not be able to assimilate and use the information in a positive way.

Thus, we underscore the belief that it is a good rule to avoid discussing your sexual past with your partner. You have absolutely nothing to gain by these disclosures—unless something in your background pertains to your present situation in a big way. Obviously, a history of sexual abuse can have an affect on your relationship. Another instance that calls for disclosure is background info that is likely to come out sooner or later—such as deviant behavior that resulted in public action, or the fact that you have worked in the sex industry. By all means, reveal anything your partner needs to know to understand you. (Always keep in mind that your partner wants to believe that your sex with him is the best you have ever experienced.)

Some couples reveal past history during fantasy talk. But be careful. It is easy to hurt your partner's feelings, and once secrets are out of the bag, you cannot take them back, and healing can take a long time. Everyone feels some inadequacies in regard to sex, and you do not want to make matters worse.

When your partner says he wants to hear about your past and thinks he can be objective, remember that he does want to hear—but he is probably not as objective as he thinks he is (especially if a prior partner of yours was a great lover). In other words, everybody wants to know the inside scoop—but few can handle what they hear. There is no predicting how your partner will receive the information, so why even go there?

45. How can I get my partner to focus on my needs during sex?

Guys are satisfied more quickly than their female counterparts. That is a given—but still, it seems hard for your partner to remember to focus on you—when he is moving at a lightning pace toward his own fulfillment.

Typically, one partner wants more focus on his needs. But what if you have trouble concentrating on your own needs and your partner's simultaneously? Doing this takes real skill in the art of lovemaking.

Also, it is unusual for both partners to enjoy the same types of stimulation and share the same sexual fantasies. Usually, in making love, you do what you like. And, if you are considerate of your partner, you do what you think the other person will enjoy, based on past experiences with him and with former partners. But what would really give you the best sex?

You should make love in a way that satisfies both of you, but the bottom line is that *you* are responsible for getting your own needs met. Tell your partner what you enjoy, and physically steer him in the right direction. But always try to be extremely tactful.

Unfortunately, most couples are not direct, so they do not get what they need. People who are eloquent speakers out of bed tend to clam up and become self-conscious when it comes to asking for what they want in bed. While you may think you will only sound demanding by telling your partner what you want, the reverse is true: He would prefer to know rather than have to fumble around—and he will definitely find it sexy hearing you talk about what you want in bed.

Reveal your preferences during lovemaking because that is when people are most receptive to that kind of input. Say what you like and want and ask your partner what he likes and needs. If you think your needs will seem unusual to your partner, go slowly. You can express yourself fully over time.

For the greatest sexual satisfaction, you must be willing to reveal your preferences and accept your partner's.

46. Is there a way to refuse sex without hurting my partner's feelings?

Not tonight, honey. Those are the words no one wants to hear—and everyone fears. Instantly, when your partner turns away from you, waves of rejection wash over you. Although you would not be fazed by your spouse's refusal of a second helping at the table, or when he is not in the mood for a movie, the subject of sexual "rejection" is a virtual land mine.

Start out with a common-sense premise that goes like this: No matter how intense your lovemaking, you will not be in the mood for sex all of the time—and neither will your mate. Agree that you will be affected by stress, illness, conflict, fatigue, depression, and fluctuations in mood. Psychological issues, medications, poor body image, and sex discomfort are others factor that sometimes decrease libido.

So, you must trust your partner and the love you share, and work on understanding what your partner is feeling in the sexual arena. The depth of sexual intimacy you can achieve is directly proportional to your ability to achieve openness. Good communication is essential.

Unfortunately, discussions of sex make most people nervous. Only time and trust and love can help you feel more relaxed talking about intimacy. You accept and respect your partner's needs so that his reluctance to have sex will not cause you to worry and second-guess his reasons.

When you want time alone, you should be able to ask for it and know that your mate will not feel abandoned. (Just cushion the blow with words of reassurance.)

47. How can we recapture the level of passion we shared originally?

Steamy, hot passion. Wet, deep kisses. Rapture unlimited.

This is probably what brought you together in the beginning. And while months and years may have cooled your perspective and fogged your priorities, that same electrical charge between you still exists, no matter how seldom you choose to draw on it.

To keep passion alive, you must both make this a priority. It is far too easy to let jobs, children, stress, and fatigue take precedence.

Interestingly, the key to restoring passion is primarily in the mind and in the heart, not in the body. Never forget that arousal stems mainly from your brain. That is why couples who address the mental process of desire can create the most change.

When you assess your sex life, you are talking about how to enhance the erotic excitement in your minds—not how to improve physical technique.

Everyone has the innate capacity for sexual arousal. But the erotic desires stimulated by intimacy are what excite us to want passionate sex. Committed partners can nurture these desires.

Using your imagination is one powerful way to rediscover passion. Explore together and alone what turns you on, and add innovations to your lovemaking. Certain types of clothes, foods, aromas, movies, touches, sounds, and settings can push our erotic buttons.

Tell your mate what arouses you. Plan romantic events, and do things differently. Remind your partner what you love about his body and what excites you. Never stop telling him how attractive he is to you and how he turns you on. Simply by sharing specifics, you can enhance passion immensely.

Keep creative juices flowing and use your imagination to reignite the spark that first brought you together. You can keep the attraction alive forever if you center the focus on satisfying each other.

48. How can massage enhance desire?

You can recharge your relationship with intimate touch—something that both of you will both find fun and exciting. Stimulate your partner by caressing, cuddling, embracing, stroking. Through erotic massage, you provide sensual pleasure that is quite different from that achieved by ordinary massage.

Though we all hunger for touch, couples sometimes ignore the desire for tactile stimulation for long periods of time. If you do not use touch, you can actually lose sensitivity to it. But you will find it easy to learn how to massage erotically, and then you can take turns pleasuring each other.

It all starts with a cozy room. Turn down the lights, and play up the ambiance with scented candles and romantic music. In your hands, warm a small amount of oil, body lotion, or baby oil scented with ylang-ylang, jasmine, or musk. (You can buy premixed sensual mixtures at a bath shop.) Ask your partner to lie on his stomach, and begin massaging his entire body. Tell him to relax and enjoy the sensations. Use a light, sensual touch—not the firm touch of regular massage. Vary the pressure, but keep it light, using your finger tips. You can even use a feather and alternate it with the sensation of your fingernails.

For variations on the basic technique, read a book on sensual massage. Learn, practice, and experiment to see what works.

49. Is it unhealthy for me to fantasize about some-one other than my partner?

Even the word fantasy conjures up interesting erotic pictures. Many fantasies are rooted in early sexual experiences, and other are borne later in life. But the bottom line is that fantasizing about other people is normal. Making love with someone other than your partner is one of the most common fantasies for both men and women.

When looking at fantasies, you need to remember that a sexual fantasy should not be regarded necessarily as a sexual wish. Rather, it is a mental aphrodisiac. The truth is, plenty of healthy, open-minded people have all sorts of fantasies, but few want to act out those that involve other people. Thinking about such things, on the other hand, is often considered fair game.

Some people, however, consider it immoral to fantasize about romantic encounters with someone other than a marital partner. This kind of guilt is often engendered by religious or parental teachings that sex is dirty. And if both of you view fantasies in this way, then, by all means, abide by your gut feelings.

But sexual thoughts *are not* the same as cheating. So, rather than feeling guilty about fantasies or worrying about what they mean, just enjoy them. Fantasies represent creative, open thinking about sex, and they can enhance desire and arousal and your ability to reach orgasm.

For many people, fantasies play a role in masturbation, and that is one reason they are good precursors of mood-setting for sex with your partner. The fact is, fantasies frequently serve to block out thoughts that interfere with arousal, especially in women.

As a general rule, fantasies are used to broaden sexual repertoires without taking risks. Overall, many sex therapists find that women who indulge in sex fantasies have healthier attitudes about sex and are more likely to be sexually fulfilled than other women.

Fantasizing during lovemaking does not make you a pervert. In fact, fantasies about someone other than your mate can be fun, safe, and enjoyable. Typically, keeping your thoughts vaulted at the fantasy level is relatively harmless. In contrast, extramarital sexual exploits are the arenas in which many partners get hurt and marriages disintegrate.

50. What should we know about masturbation?

You did it as a kid, and, no, you did not go blind, after all. This is a normal and healthy practice indulged in by many people. We are referring to masturbation, which is self-stimulation of the genitals for sexual pleasure—an activity that often leads to orgasm. Many people (even some who will not say the word) regard masturbation as a safe way to achieve sexual release; it is simple, risk-free, and harmless. With no distractions interfering, masturbation can help you focus on erotic sensations; you do not need to concern yourself with pleasing a partner.

In our mixed-signals society, it is important for people to understand that it is all right to enjoy strong erotic physical sensations that are self-induced. You do not need to feel guilty; you can simply enjoy masturbation as an affirmation of self-love and an appreciation of the erotic aspects of your persona.

Used appropriately, it can enhance your relationship. Though usually a solitary act, it can also be performed in front of your partner. Masturbation helps you learn how your body responds to different types of stimulation. Some partners masturbate simultaneously to vary their lovemaking; the visual stimulation of watching your partner can be exciting. By being a voyeur on the sideline, you can grow your understanding of what arouses your partner

Masturbation can even help you practice sexual imagery, which will enhance your arousal and the strength of your orgasms. This action, often honed in adolescence, is sometimes used to overcome sexual problems such as impotency, premature ejaculation, or arousal problems in women. Masturbation also comes in handy for sexual release when your partner is unavailable or incapacitated.

Many people preach that masturbation is bad or that it will detract from your bond as a couple. But in committed relationships, partners should always have the right to enjoy their own bodies without feeling guilty (you are not cheating). The only way this can adversely affect a relationship is if one partner chronically binge-masturbates and withholds sex from his partner.

Essentially, many people who enjoy sex find pleasure in exploring the full range of their sexuality. If you can enjoy masturbation without guilt, you are more likely to be an uninhibited lover.

As far as frequency, that is as variable as DNA. Some people masturbate daily while others do it less frequently. The only ones who should wonder if they could be masturbating too much are those who do follow this practice in inappropriate places or situations or let it interfere with their lives or relationships.

51. How does the use of pornographic and erotic material affect a relationship?

Porn and erotica certainly are not the first things that come to mind when you think of loving relationships. Both terms have shady connotations, in fact. Pornography refers to very explicit sexual art, pictures, movies, and literature, and erotica encompasses writings that deal with explicit descriptions of sexual love.

But, the truth is, some very normal loving pairs are highly aroused by these unusual forms of literature, writings, art, etc. Arousing materials definitely help some people achieve sexual gratification, and, for that reason, they have become commonplace in sex therapy.

How does it work? Pornography and erotica are used to expand sexual repertoires and teach people how to be considerate lovers. These forms of media can also enhance arousal. The most common scenarios are that males are excited by visual expressions of sex, while women tend to prefer erotic materials with a romantic story and sexually explicit descriptions.

Usually, if you are secure with your sexuality, you are more likely to be accepting of pornographic and erotic materials (the explicitness does not feel threatening). You may use these materials as a prelude to lovemaking to increase arousal. Many couples watch porn videos together, and some like to read erotic literature. But, proceed with caution if you are venturing into this realm for the first time; do not pressure your partner into viewing erotic material. If you are the only one turned on by the material, keep it to yourself. And when selecting movies, favor those with romantic themes over the ones with violent and degrading images, which have no value in promoting intimacy.

Erotica is exciting; view it as a positive adventure. Accept each other's tastes and find a balance that satisfies your individual needs and the needs of the relationship.

52. Right now my partner thinks I am sexy and desirable—can this last?

When the two of you first met, you knew your partner had the hots for you. Every time you saw each other, carnal oblivion hit, and soon you were locked in a mad embrace, tumbling toward the bedroom.

But that was then and this is now. What can you do to make sure that your partner will continue to find you sexy? Believe it or not, this is something you can control to some extent. You simply have to act sexy, feel sexy, and believe you are sexy. Attitude and confidence are huge. Appearance, dress, speech, movement, and mannerisms are components, too, but you can definitely be sexy without being gorgeous or having a perfect body. Focus on your good qualities.

One of the most important areas is body image. To have good sex, you need to love your body. Start improving your diet, exercising more, and updating your makeup. Experiment with ways of feeling more sensual. Change your fragrance or the color of your hair. Wear seductive clothing, or very little at all.

Most importantly, work on your mind. Explore erotic thoughts. Write love letters to your partner. Ponder how wild you really are. Be openly affectionate, physically and verbally. Talk sexy to your partner.

When your partner senses that you feel desirable, he will respond. Praise him for his sexy attributes, and he will reciprocate. When you get in touch with your sexy side as well as your partner's, it is bound to enhance the relationship.

53. How can we get rid of sexual inhibitions?

The dishrag woman. The stuffed-shirt man. We have come across them, but we cannot truthfully say that we have loved them in bed. A wild-and-crazy lover is more fun any day, but some people have no idea how to get there.

Many of us are embarrassed or closed-minded about certain sexual practices due to parental or religious influences, culture, or poor sex education. The most common inhibitions have to do with modesty about nudity or reticence to perform sex acts that do not seem clean or safe.

For an inhibited person, being passionate and erotic is totally out of the question because it produces anxiety, which limits sexual expression and strains the relationship. Inhibited couples are not intimate.

To overcome sexual inhibition, discuss any behavior you are nervous about. After that, reeducate yourself with facts—and try desensitization. Partners should bolster each other's image because someone who feels desirable is in a better position to overcome stumbling blocks.

Some tips for freeing yourself of inhibitions: Learn to feel good about your body. Know your sexual anatomy. Masturbate to discover what makes you feel good.

Having your partner enjoy your body and sensually pleasure you will lead to a new level of openness. A partner who engages in sexual activities in a loving, relaxed manner encourages the inhibited partner to feel more comfortable with forms of sexual activity he once dreaded. For example, you can easily overcome a fear of oral sex with the help of an uninhibited, relaxed partner. Talking sexy during lovemaking will help relax you and get you more "into" the feared behavior.

To experience new levels of intimacy, share your fears and confront them. With proper guidance, inhibited individuals can become confident, skilled lovers who can give and receive erotic pleasure without anxiety.

54. If I have same-sex fantasies, does that mean I am homosexual in orientation?

You are female, but you can easily see why your fiancé thinks your room-mate is a goddess. Or maybe you are a guy who thinks his girlfriend's brother is handsome. Perhaps, these gorgeous creatures have even sneaked into your mind when you were masturbating or having sex with your partner.

You do not need to worry that your sexual orientation is slipping so that you are entering a different genre. These common scenarios do not make you a homosexual. Sexual fantasies—erotic thoughts that serve as mental aphrodisiacs—are healthy expressions of imagination that can be used to improve desire and arousal over and over again. In fact, women who fanta-size actively are usually better adjusted sexually and more satisfied.

Sometimes, fantasies are fleeting thoughts; other times, they are detailed and visually graphic. Content varies, depending on the couple's erotic interests, experiences, background, and willingness to be open to unusual areas of sexuality.

At any rate, it is important to remember that few people really want to act out fantasies—and fantasies about sex with members of your own gender are common in both men and women (although men are reluctant to admit it). Same-sex fantasies have nothing to do with biological sexual orientation.

Most people who are open-minded enough to have such fantasies sim-ply wonder what it would be like to pleasure someone who is similar anatomically and has similar responses. And even if you do act out a same-sex fantasy and find the contact enjoyable, that still does not mean you're homosexual. You are still what you are, homosexual or heterosexual, based on your innate attraction to the same or opposite sex. Men fear that it is a sign of latent homosexuality, and women may worry about their leanings, but your basic sexual orientation does not change, regardless of fantasies or same-sex contact.

The more forbidden the subject, the more likely it is to evoke sexual fantasies in bright, open-minded people. Rather than feeling guilty, enjoy your thoughts and allow them to enhance masturbation or sex with your partner. The broader your repertoire of fantasies, the more exciting your sexuality, if only in your mind.

55. How should partners deal with temptation?

The world is full of beautiful, sexy people—and some of them are in your neighborhood, your church or synagogue, and your workplace. These are tempting scenarios, especially when one of these attractive people makes overtures. He wants you—and that feels good. It makes you feel alive, especially if your mate has been taking you for granted.

Basically, absolutely anyone who has a healthy, open attitude about sex is likely to face sexual attractions—even when he already has a strong relationship. These feelings are normal, and it shows that desire and arousal are still alive and well within that individual.

But, typically, fleeting attractions fade. Until they do, you can simply experience them and use them to stimulate sexual thoughts. You do not have to act on them. And you should not feel guilty for being normal; just let the feelings die a natural death as time passes.

Generally, allowing a temptation to damage your relationship is incredibly foolish. Eventually, you will be left with nothing but memories, both of your temptress and your spouse. Passing attractions can last weeks or months, but sustaining a loving partnership requires focus, effort, and commitment. Temptation is a part of life. View it for what is it and what it means, and it loses much of its power. Summon up the courage to make the right choice so that you will not damage your committed relationship. Have no doubt—intimacy can be lost. You must decide if a passing fancy is important enough to jeopardize a stable intimate relationship.

56. Is seduction a two-way street?

You can be the sexiest vamp your partner ever came across. In turn, he can be your eternal Brad Pitt. Seduction definitely works best when both partners take an active role. You do not want to be the sole initiator. And, if you expect your partner to make all the overtures, he will resent it (plus, you will seem unexciting).

Our attitudes about seduction and sex are spawned in childhood, when we are influenced by family, religion, learned morals, sexual experiences, and romantic readings. Women are often conditioned to be passive; in other words, they think men should make the advances. Some men even regard sexually aggressive women as unhealthy and overzealous.

However, in an intimate relationship, both partners should share the excitement of seducing, attracting, and arousing. If you worry about rejection or if you fear expressing your sexual side, confront these issues and deal with them.

When partners are comfortable expressing carnal impulses, it provides a solid foundation of trust, from which intimacy can blossom. Mutual pleasuring is essential in maintaining closeness.

57. Should we share our sexual fantasies?

Do wild fantasies mean that you are perverted, your head reeling with bizarre scenarios? And how did such corruption get into the head of a nice, normal person like you?

In fact, vivid sexual fantasies serve many purposes, and the only time they are negatives is when they interfere with intimacy in a relationship. Commonly, partners feel conflicted about sharing fantasies with their partner, so it is your job to determine how you think your partner will react. The onus is on you. Can he handle knowing that you imagine sexual activity with others? He might find the idea exciting (certainly, many people do). Or he might be offended and jealous (also, many people do).

Often, sharing fantasies adds excitement to lovemaking, particularly if you keep an open mind. But consider your partner. In some cases, it is simply better to keep your fantasies private.

If your partner's fantasies fail to excite you, you can still be tolerant and accepting. Expressing a fantasy has a more powerful effect than holding it in.

58. Are there legal aphrodisiacs that enhance sexual desire?

We have all heard of aphrodisiacs since junior-high days. Wondered about them. Maybe even tried some of them. But what is real—do they actually work?

It is common knowledge that people can buy substances long touted for enhancing sexual desire. These are available illegally and legally, with and without a prescription. But, the truth is, no substance that is now sold legally enhances sexual desire or arousal in most people. Aphrodisiacs have a placebo effect. If you believe it is going to work, it will. Since the brain is the primary sex organ, you simply fool the brain into thinking that you will feel hotter, that something erotic will take place. A placebo can have the desired result, but the substance consumed will not be responsible.

Nevertheless, some people believe in the erotic powers of certain foods, drinks, herbs, and substances derived from various parts of animals (such as rhino tusks). There are those who like the effects of ginseng, saw palmetto, ginkgo, and yohimbe, a substance sold in health-food stores that is supposed to help men keep an erection through its effect on blood flow. Some cultures swear by oysters, ginseng, alcohol, and chocolate, all of which have worked on occasion. But, none of these are universally effective, and none have been proven in studies.

Caveats: Those who want to experiment should remember that any substance can have idiosyncratic side effects that can be harmful—so be cautious. And most products sold to enhance desire and arousal are disappointing. That is true unless you want to rely on the placebo effect, which, with enough hype, will make any substance seem stimulating.

Sexual hormones such as testosterone and estrogen and progesterone do have a scientific basis for working in those with lower-than-normal hormone levels. Viagra helps men have erections and maintain them—and even enhances blood flow to women's genitals, making that area more responsive to touch. This medication does not affect sexual desire or arousal except in an indirect way, though it has very positive effects on the end result of arousal.

Illegal drugs such as cocaine do have direct effects on the centers of the brain that stimulate sexual desire and arousal, but the downsides to your health and welfare are far too enormous to make this a viable choice.

Some essential oils, by inducing a relaxing sensual effect when inhaled or absorbed through the skin during massage or bath, enhance desire. Also, there are perfumes and odors known to have a sensual effect.

Eventually, companies will market drugs that consumers can use to increase sexual desire and arousal. Pharmaceutical companies are working to find the substance that will bring about the desired response without significant side effects.

Currently, though, no chemical substance can rival the powerful aphrodisiac effect of good health, regular exercise, and loving behavior.

59. Do nice girls use sex toys?

Vibrators are the butt of comedians' jokes—as well as the number-one sex toy sold in America.

Today, the use of sex toys is on the upswing because they are more readily available in shops, catalogs, and over the Internet. Men used to be the main consumers, but now women, too, are buying vibrators, dildos, feathers, whips, paddles, restraints, ben wa balls, nipple clamps, and S&M toys. Also available are items of erotic apparel, and massage oils and lubricants used for penetration.

People looking for new turn-ons often experiment with sex toys although roadblocks still stand in the way of widespread acceptance. Many women associate sex toys with kinky sex and assume that only "naughty girls" use them. Others believe that vibrators or dildos provide unnatural gratification, so these are immoral devices. But those who are less judgmental often discover new ways to explore their bodies, thus enhancing their sex lives.

Drugstores sell vibrators that are marketed as "personal body massagers," and these battery-powered devices allow women to explore their anatomy and discover the different feelings generated by touching certain spots. These help women become orgasmic more easily because vibrators intensely stimulate the clitoral area, which facilitates orgasms in women who have had difficulty in the past.

Clearly, there seems to be no harm in having fun, being adventurous, and experimenting with different toys. Each has its own unique sensation. The bottom line is that you do not need to feel ashamed about pleasuring yourself and your partner; keeping your sex life interesting is a good idea, always.

60. What is the best way to deal with differences in sex drive?

He is always reading statistics on "normal" numbers of times that married couples have intercourse per week. She is big on showing him surveys in women's magazines that beg to differ. For him, every morning and night would be about right. For her, once a month is overkill.

One partner thinks his needs are being ignored; the other feels like she is living with a sex addict. It is a tricky problem. You want a solution, but you do not want either partner to come to view sex as a chore.

In cases of sexual incompatibility, first consider the possibility of a physical problem. Then, see if you have different ideas; one person might prefer quantity of sex while the other prefers quality less often. As a side issue, make sure that your increased sex drive really is, in fact, an increased need for sex because sometimes, partners who feel neglected, ignored, or unloved will demand sex. The other partner will push the demander away, and the demanding partner will escalate sexual demands even more.

Two people who are in love should be willing to compromise. Discuss your beliefs, physical needs, and means of satisfying those. List similarities and differences. Then use this information to work out a compromise. Besides intercourse, there are other ways, such as masturbation, to satisfy needs. Another option: ask your partner for more limited but satisfying stimulation.

Differences in physical needs and approaches to lovemaking do not preclude your being in love. A strong desire to make the relationship work means you will find a solution to the problem of differences in drive. Give each other options.

61. How important are touching, caressing, and foreplay?

Foreplay has gotten a bad rap. Some men find it comical—because it is something women fixate on (males have less need for a warm-up). Women think it is important to their sexual gratification—and also because it is indicative of how selfless the man is. If he does not want to bother with foreplay (i.e., making her feel good), how good a partner will he be in sharing life?

Without foreplay, you can have sex, but you will miss the erotic aspects of superior lovemaking in that sensual overtures can be a vital part of two lovers' physical contact. In essence, foreplay can be thought of as the foundation for emotionally meaningful lovemaking. Touching, especially sensual touching, conveys the erotic spirit that is in the hearts of loving partners. Of course, you can have sex minus the foreplay because desire and arousal can be generated within the mind prior to physical contact, but the deepest levels of arousal will elude you.

All too often, partners fail to get each other in an erotic mood before making love. During courtship, when partners are fully into the exhilaration of the preliminaries, touching and caressing are almost always used to enhance intimacy. But after the relationship ripens, the time spent enjoying these fringe benefits usually shrinks, as couple dynamics change with the demands of busy schedules, children, and revised priorities.

It is not unusual for married couples to grow increasingly indifferent to each other's needs. Soon, the time between onset of sex play and orgasm is shortened to the bare minimum. Foreplay is bypassed in favor of rapid orgasmic release.

At the same time, it is important for couples to remember the value of foreplay; sensual, affectionate, and erotic touching makes both partners feel aroused and loved. Those who argue that sex should be exclusively penetration-and-orgasm usually neglect the prelims, and many end up dissatisfied.

What makes sex true lovemaking is complete focus—when two people give one another total erotic attention, which means fully experiencing the flow of sexual energy. Gazing in each other's eyes with loving passion, they enjoy touching and being touched, and they achieve intimacy and satisfaction.

62. How a man can learn to delay his orgasms?

Few would disagree that orgasm is an incredible high. The end-all and be-all of sexuality. And that begs the question: Why don't people understand orgasms and what it takes to reach them?

Orgasms—sensations brought about by sexual arousal—are usually experienced as a series of rhythmic contractions triggered by intense physical and psychological sexual stimulation. Typically, an orgasm lasts from a few seconds to 20 seconds or more, with genital sensations lasting several minutes in some people.

Since the orgasm is the pleasurable culmination of sexual stimulation, it has historically been a strong focus of writers and scientists—and this has resulted in a great deal of emphasis on learning to control the timing of orgasm. In some situations, couples want to delay orgasm to allow a buildup of arousal so that both experience maximum satisfaction, ensuring that the female partner is satisfied before her mate loses his erection. Other times, a fast orgasm is the straightforward goal.

Experts advance many strategies for delaying male orgasm, accelerating female orgasm, and enhancing the quality of the orgasm in both. These have been developed by tantric priests in India and by western sex therapists. But, the truth is, people differ widely in patterns and needs when it comes to orgasm. Usually, the male is quick to reach orgasm, while a female requires more stimulation. This means men usually need to learn how to delay orgasm until their female partners have sufficient arousal for orgasm. Of course, many women also achieve orgasm via other means.

It is generally agreed that an active sex life is the key to being orgasmic throughout life. Orgasms release sexual tension and decrease general irritability, which makes the benefits of regular orgasms very real, both physically and psychologically. You are left with a feeling of well-being and relaxation. You know that you need to "come" when a buildup of sexual tension spawns a preoccupation with sexual thinking, which signals need.

Both partners validate their sexuality by their ability (or inability) to have a satisfying orgasm. Some women never reach orgasm by stimulation during lovemaking; they always require direct clitoral stimulation. Others need self-stimulation during masturbation. About 30 percent of women reach orgasm through intercourse only.

As women age, they seem to become more responsive to reaching the level of arousal that induces orgasm. In men, the main concern is delaying orgasm to allow for satisfying intercourse. But it is easy to treat men who have trouble with premature ejaculation, which is common.

Men can learn to delay orgasm by varying their thrust pattern during intercourse. You have more control when you vary the depth of the thrust, as well as speed and power. Another technique: Stop thrusting when you feel the point of ejaculation fast approaching. Pull back to about an inch of penetration; do not withdraw. Contract your pelvic muscles for five to 10 seconds, then resume with shallow thrusting.

Another technique: Alternate lovemaking technique. When you are highly aroused, stop thrusting, withdraw, and stimulate your partner orally or manually. When you are back in control, resume penetration.

Varying mental imagery while thrusting can help control your state of arousal. When you want to increase your arousal, conjure up erotic images. When you want to decrease arousal, think less stimulating thoughts.

Another technique is a perineum press: Before you reach the point of ejaculation, use three curved fingers to apply pressure to the perineum between the scrotum and anus. Practice during masturbation to find the exact spot and right amount of pressure. These techniques can delay the male orgasm and increase overall satisfaction.

For women, reaching orgasm faster is usually the goal. You can achieve this by having your partner find the right kind of stimulation to achieve maximum arousal.

It also helps to relax and focus on sensations and fantasies. Too often, women concentrate too much on having an orgasm (instead, just enjoy the feelings). The more you focus on the orgasm, the more you delay it.

V

Trust/Insecurities

63. How can we learn to trust each other?

A million songs have been written about cheating hearts. And an equal number of movies and books. Little wonder, we spend way too much time sorting out this difficult topic.

Trust is a foundation for a satisfying relationship, but it is also a complex matter. You must share your inner self, knowing all the while that your partner will respect your vulnerabilities, safeguard your confidences, and respond to your concerns. It requires honesty and dependability.

To trust, you must believe that you are deeply loved and that your partner's primary concerns are you and the relationship. You should not need constant reminders that your partner treasures you, but in a good relationship, you will get many reminders along the way. Reinforcing behaviors make partners feel secure.

Real trust allows you to relax, with no need to be vigilant. You do not have to worry that the other will let you down. Your partner loves you, is there for you forever, and will support the sanctity of the relationship, no matter what.

The more trusting the relationship, the greater the payoffs in security, closeness, and intimacy. A lack of trust can stem from insecurity—you harbor concerns that your partner could abandon you at anytime. There are many reasons to feel this way, and it is important to figure out the source of your misgivings so that you can work toward full trust. One major reason for lack of trust is a heartbreaking loss or broken trust in the past; now you are suspicious of everyone, no matter how trustworthy. In such cases, you need to work through past hurts so that you can experience trust with future partners. Discuss your feelings with a close friend or therapist. Otherwise, you will carry over past feelings and attach them to present and future partners.

Another reason for a lack of trust is low self-image. You do not believe your partner can love you. Childhood failed to leave you with a positive view of yourself. The solution? Take a good look at yourself and appreciate what your partner sees in you. If they see it, it is there; try to have faith in what they see.

Obviously, if your partner is not loving and does not seem truthful (based on things you can verify), there is reason to be distrustful. This usually requires couples counseling. Start with calm, open discussions of what you think is happening before you progress to formal counseling. You need to pinpoint what is actually behind your lack of trust.

64. Is it a given that the abuse in my past will hurt my current relationship?

You may have trouble bonding with a partner if you have had mental, physical, or sexual abuse as a child or an adult. This does not preclude the possibility of true intimacy, but a healthy relationship will take hard work.

Certainly, the degree of abuse, age, and type of abuse are critical factors. So are the compassion, understanding, and love provided by your present partner. You are also hampered or helped by your family attitude toward sexuality, your childhood relationships, your healthy sexual history, and positive experiences with people you have trusted.

Abuse results in fragile self-esteem. Spinoffs are:

- You feel unworthy of love.
- Your trust tends to be weak, and you question motives for closeness and whether your partner really loves you.
- You have mood swings and anxiety when your partner gets too close, too sexual, or too distant.
- You have difficulty dealing with intense emotions toward your partner.
- You may experience blocked or anxiety-producing sexual feelings that cause you to avoid sex.
- You find that today's experiences can reactivate old feelings unrelated to your present relationship or partner.

Despite all of these blocks, you can grow more confident of deserving love and overcome uneasy feelings if your partner is loving, understanding, trustworthy, and patient. It is important to express your vulnerabilities and fears. Be patient and let the strengths in your relationship help you relax, let go of the past, and enjoy true intimacy.

65. How should I handle the fact that my partner flirts?

Most people like to think they are attractive to people other than just their partner, which can give rise to flirting. But, flirtatious behavior is not a threat if your relationship has a solid foundation; if you have a good self-image; and if you feel secure in your partner's love for you. If you are not secure in yourself or the relationship and this kind of behavior bothers you, discuss the matter in a calm manner. Do not take a possessive, jealous position.

Also ask yourself: Is this really a problem or am I blowing it out of proportion? Are you normally a very romantic, intimate couple? Is sex a problem? Is your partner really trying to make new intimate friends? Consider these issues and work on them.

Flirting may be a symptom of something significantly wrong with relationship, or you may be misconstruing things because you are not sure how your partner feels about you or you do not trust him. Figure out if the flirting is destructive and needs to be changed; then decide what the change should be. To do this, you must analyze the basis for your feelings and what you think the flirtatious behavior means.

Some people actually enjoy watching how others respond when their partner flirts. Watching other people flirt back can be an erotic turn-on.

At any rate, deciding what to do about flirtatious behavior may be vital for your relationship to flourish. Just keep in mind that you are the one your partner goes to bed with every night—and most cases of casual flirting are harmless.

66. What is normal (and abnormal) when it comes to jealousy?

That little' ol' green-eyed monster—jealousy—we all have a little of it in us. But some people have way too much—enough to spoil a relationship.

Jealousy stems from insecurity, which, in turn, results from low self-esteem. A jealous person fears that the relationship is being threatened and fights feelings of helplessness with accusations that harm the relationship.

When a partner feels insecure, he tries to demean and/or control his mate. And someone who is overly dependent may even be jealous of a partner's achievements.

As an untamed element in a relationship, jealousy can lead to anger and hostility and cause enormous rifts. The partner under attack pulls away and stops sharing his achievements. Both partners become isolated, breeding more suspicion.

In a good relationship, each partner must develop a sense of self and enjoy work, hobbies, body, and mind. Neither individual needs to be defined by a mate. If partners have good self-esteem and take pride in their own achievements, it is very unlikely that jealousy will be problematic. (Bear in mind that a little jealousy is normal while a great deal can be destructive.)

67. How can we keep from worrying about sexual infidelity?

The thought of your spouse making love with someone else can eat you alive. And the reality can make you psychotic. Most of us really do not understand this volatile subject, but we should believe that it is potent, considering the fact that cheating sometimes leads to murder.

It is quite normal to be concerned about disloyalty. This usually stems from feelings of insecurity, and it may be based on absolutely nothing concrete that your partner has done. Other times, one partner may feel that he has picked up clues.

When two people want a relationship to work, they must let go of suspicion that will hurt them and the relationship. When you know that you and your partner love each other and share a happy life, you put aside accusations, suspicions, and condemnation, and you focus on what is real, not imagined.

When couples allow fears about infidelity to interfere with a successful relationship, they begin behaving in destructive ways. Sometimes, one partner is making the other feel insecure, breeding worry. The insecure partner obsesses on imagined infidelities and agonizes over real or imagined flirtations. The relationship starts to weaken. The partner who feels betrayed searches for clues to confirm his suspicions. Usually, it is possible to read betrayal in all kinds of actions and clues. If you find anything that suggests your suspicions are on target, regardless of actual facts, anxiety increases even when your partner can prove there is no basis in fact. Finally, you are incapacitated by worry, jealousy, and insecurity.

Partners who feel secure in their relationships and themselves are less apt to experience irrational jealousy. Feelings of doubt diminish when you learn to be less dependent, have more faith in your relationship, and focus on the real over the imagined.

When you do feel suspicious and jealous, examine the relationship and yourself. Determine what this signifies and where the feelings are coming from.

- Does the relationship need a jump start sexually?
- Is there a need to work on building intimacy?
- Why is trust lacking?
- Is there boredom on both sides?
- Are you depressed?
- Is there a hormonal imbalance due to aging or pregnancy?
- Are you feeling insecure?

Improve your self-esteem so you do not need to rely on your partner for self-worth. When both partners feel good about themselves and the relationship, there is no reason to imagine infidelities. Focus on positives.

68. Will my confidence level and self-image affect our intimacy?

When you have a healthy, positive self-image, you feel good about yourself and, in turn, feel good about being loved. A person who is confident is more desirable. If you do not value yourself and your abilities, you seem inferior because you act like you feel that way. You are very likely to be defensive, sensitive, and jealous.

Your image also determines your happiness about life in general, and this affects your intimate relationship. Low self-esteem means you will not accept criticism, and you will have trouble problem-solving. Anytime you and your partner disagree, it is very important to you to prove that you are right.

More problems crop up when you try to boost your shaky ego by criticizing your partner. This spills over into public disagreements that damage the relationship.

If you feel good about yourself, you are more relaxed and loving, and, in turn, your partner is tender and loving. You feel like you deserve the best; in turn, you get the best. A confident person rarely tolerates unhealthy or unloving behavior.

Basically, a good self-image makes you interesting, exciting, and irresistible to your partner because you exude confidence, grace, style, and poise. You are at peace with yourself and with those around you.

69. Can we regain intimacy after trust is broken?

A betrayed partner, even after a period of healing and good times, is often waiting for the other shoe to drop. Learning to trust again is difficult, but far from impossible.

It is very important to share responsibility for a broken trust; your "relationship" failed in order for the infraction to take place, but the one who did the act must accept greater responsibility for making a conscious choice to violate trust. The partner who was wronged must let go of his need to condemn and entertain the idea of forgiveness. The violator must take steps to show his renewed commitment to the relationship and seek to instill trust again. This can include sincere apologies, refocusing attention on his partner, improved listening, special trips, increased dependability. And both partners can work on improving communication and closeness, hoping to stave off future breaches. Finally, forgiveness by the wronged party is a huge step forward.

If you love each other and think that you are meant to be together, you must be willing to trust with your entire heart. If you search for evidence of disloyalty, you will be suspicious of everything your partner does. And if you fail to give your mate the benefit of the doubt, he will feel like he is under attack. He will also resent persistent mistrust and be slow to offer reassurances. Tired of scrutiny, he may become evasive. Knowing that you will not believe what he says, he embroiders on the truth, saying what he thinks you want to hear. This only adds to inconsistencies in his story and leads to more doubt on your part.

Bottom line: The more you mistrust, the more you create a context where there is reason to continue mistrusting. Trust requires a leap of faith, and you cannot wait until you feel trusting to start. Be willing to forgive and move forward, even though you will definitely have highs and lows. Remain secure in your own desirability and worthiness, and when your partner makes efforts to change, express appreciation.

You can learn to trust again by rebuilding the bond of intimacy you once shared. Together, you can overcome your fears. You won't forget past hurts, but you can forgive them—and move on.

70. How should we handle broken promises?

You cannot have true intimacy unless you trust your partner. Keeping promises shows your integrity and your respect for yourself and others. Casually making promises without any concern for keeping them makes your partner realize that your word is suspect and he can't believe anything you say. Failing to fulfill commitments tells your partner that he can't count on you in the future.

Some people promise things without knowing whether they can deliver. They have been disappointed frequently and do not mind letting down others. Their word means little.

It is important to make your commitments count. Never promise anything without making a sincere effort to uphold your word. Good relationships are built on honesty, dependability, and reliability.

71. *Is honesty always best?*

You trust your partner to do the right thing and be honest in behaviors and feelings. Honesty means not hiding the truth.

It is important to remember that lying will drain the life out of a relationship and destroy trust. Your bonds of intimacy will be weakened.

Does this mean you should tell your partner everything? You tell the truth in a way that doesn't injure, which can be difficult at times. You know what to tell your partner and when. Honest and sensitive communication are cornerstones of a committed relationship.

72. *How can I learn to accept my body?*

Out of shape? Overweight? Not-what-you-used-to-be?

If you think your body could look better, you are in sync with most of the American population. Everybody feels that way. At the same time, you need to work on a faltering body image, because this is an important part of a satisfying relationship. When you think you look sexy, you feel sexy, and your partner finds you desirable.

Unfortunately, we live in a society that idolizes youth, beauty, and physical perfection. Cosmetic surgery is booming because men and women want to look like the perfect images they see in the media (where even gorgeous models are touched up). In this crazy world, it is not unusual for women to have poor body images even though, to others, they look good. Often, a woman with an attractive, sexy body won't want her partner to see her nude because she is embarrassed that she is imperfect. She cannot lose herself in wild, passionate loving because she fixates on areas of her body that she fears will repulse her partner.

You may, indeed, have a poor body image, but you can resolve to improve it. Here are tips on accepting yourself:

• Assess your positives.

- Focus on what is good about your body.
- Remind yourself that you do not have to be perfect to be sexy and attractive. Many gorgeous women with physical shortcomings are sexy.
- Remember that confidence and sex appeal are compelling.
- Accept yourself as you are, and concentrate on being passionate and loving.
- Let go of unrealistic standards.
- Remind yourself that your partner finds you attractive the way you are (not the way you think you should be).
- Stop comparing yourself to others.
- If there are ways you can make yourself more attractive, work on them if you want to. Improve muscle tone and lose weight through exercise and dieting. Have your teeth cleaned. Dress in a more flattering manner to play up your strengths. Improve your hairstyle and makeup.
- Visualize yourself looking sexy and attractive. Smile. Try to see yourself as your partner sees you. Embrace yourself as a desirable person who is worthy of love.

73. Even though I have a shaky self-image, can I gain my partner's respect?

Exuding confidence makes you lovable. If you lack a good self-image, you probably come across as a weak and unassertive person who can be easily manipulated. You try to bolster your sense of worth by giving in, trying to please others.

A person with a weak self-image, teamed with a partner who has a controlling personality, is in for trouble because the stronger individual may exploit the weaker partner, who feels helpless and frustrated.

Another problem is that a lack of self-esteem can keep you from taking the steps necessary to achieve goals that will make you happy. You may give up too soon. Once you learn to trust your ability to influence the course of your life, you will earn the respect of others.

74. How can we keep from dwelling on the past?

Couples spend countless, unproductive hours rehashing old hurts. It turns into a destructive pattern; one of you lashes out, and the other reacts by doing the same. If you are with anyone long enough, there will always be some troubled water under the bridge. But you do not have to keep dredging it up.

Obsessing about what your partner has done in the past keeps a partnership stagnant. Repeating the same arguments over and over destroys intimacy, slowly but surely. Negative patterns develop. When you live in the past, you react to old, unresolved feelings rather than to the situation at hand.

The answer comes in forgiving your partner and yourself for hurts. You make a conscious choice to move forward with renewed strength and knowledge learned from the past, and you gain tremendous relief, peace, and comfort. Finally, you are living in the present, no longer languishing in anger and self-pity.

We fear letting go of past hurts because we wonder whether these things will happen again. Have the issues been discussed enough?

But you will find it very liberating to move on, knowing you have learned from the past but you are not controlled by it. By escaping destructive patterns and reacting to today's situations based on current considerations alone, you strengthen communication and trust.

75. *What is the best way to show sensitivity to each other's insecurities?*

Sarcasm. Indifference. Thoughtlessness. These can take all the oomph out of relationships. If you cannot show sensitivity and compassion, though you claim to be committed to someone, how can you expect to survive bouts of doubt, fear, and insecurity?

To make the partnership solid, you must try to understand your partner and accept him. Hiding shortcomings compromises intimacy. You cannot be deeply connected with someone whom you don't know and understand.

You must be able to express who you truly are and what you really feel. Acceptance and understanding are cornerstones of this process. You both must be able to reveal yourselves, knowing that you will be protected, loved, and appreciated. Naturally, people will simply retreat if they think they are being unfairly judged, criticized. When you allow access to your innermost thoughts and feelings, no matter how irrational or silly, you must feel safe and accepted.

To be empathetic, you must experience your partner's concerns in the same way he does. Get on the same wavelength and see a situation through his eyes to gain greater understanding of his insecurities. You know, understand, and support your partner; and he does the same for you.

VI

Romance/Friendship

76. Is friendship an absolute necessity in an intimate relationship?

For intimacy, partners must be friends and lovers. The greater the friendship, the greater the loving feelings. You like each other, enjoy being together, and have fun sharing experiences.

This does not mean that the friendship should be all-consuming. You must respect your partner's separate needs—but, all the while, you know he is there for you, understands you, and cares about your thoughts and emotions.

Real intimacy and intense loving exist only in the presence of mental and spiritual bonding. Physical intimacy without meaningful friendship or companionship is nothing more than two people having sex. A partnership is not two strangers under a common roof, without shared spirit, companionship, or friendship. "Having sex" is satisfying urges. "Making love" is much more. The rewards of truly meaningful lovemaking, which come from friendship, bonding, and intimacy, bring about the deepest physical satisfaction humans can experience.

The essence of intimacy is two friends coming together as soulmates, bonded by purpose and spirit. This is easily transformed into a physical bonding of high-intensity lovemaking. Partners feel the connection in their hearts and souls. They experience a free flow of shared intimacy and love, along with intense erotic feelings, which create a unique, incomparable bond.

77. What leads to greater spontaneity in romance?

Remember the nights you danced until dawn? And what about that rapturous coupling on the stairs, two hungry bodies grappling in mad, impetuous lovemaking?

Many couples simply relegate fond memories to the scrapbook; they assume that kind of grand passion is gone forever. But some are more optimistic, longing to recapture the romance that felt so fabulous at the outset.

The truth is, no matter how long you have been together, romance is still within your grasp. All you need is a desire to please your partner and reinforce the romantic spirit of your relationship.

Most of us associate romance with courting, so it is not surprising that, after that period passes, fast-paced lives zap our motivation. Typically, we get stuck in routines that are devoid of romance

On the other hand, there are diehard romantics. Their spiritual bonding serves as a natural motivator. These couples believe in the benefits of romance.

Some people plan romantic dinners, trips—planned events that are vital for intimacy. But to perpetuate the romantic aspects of courtship, you also need romantic spontaneity. To rekindle this spirit, try some of these ideas:

* Think back to times when you were spontaneous—when sentimental, charming ways were parts of everyday life.

* Revisit courting behavior: flowers, cards, gifts, wine, candlelight dinners, sexy dressing, love songs, sweet notes, long drives, hugs, kisses, touching.

* Be a spur-of-the-moment romantic. Pop into a room just to let your partner know that he is attractive, sexy, and special. Send him an E-mail love note.

78. *Why is it important to work together in time of crisis?*

Most of us do just fine standing by someone's side during the good times. The laughter is nonstop; the money is flowing; you are rocking all night long. But how will your love hold out during times of crisis? Will your partner be there to hold your hand and support you?

Take a long look at how your partner reacts to rough periods. It takes a united front in times of turmoil, sorrow, and crisis to strengthen and empower your bond. When your partner helps you during critical times, this shows that he honors the relationship and wants a love that is enduring.

Acting together, you can turn hardships into opportunities for growth. Initially, a crisis will make you anxious. Under duress, it is hard to gather your thoughts. But, gradually, you regroup, assess the situation, and find answers.

With support and a team approach, you can both stay calm and mobilize coping skills quickly. You will not feel alone, and you will arrive at solutions.

Everyone needs support during crisis. When your partner is with you, you will express your emotions. Through venting and coping strategies, supportive couples can weather a crisis successfully. Working together, the two of you will sustain intimacy and romance for a lifetime. Partners who team up during hard times have more intense joy during peaceful times.

79. *Should our relationship be my top priority?*

Yes, definitely! But it should not be your only priority. An intimate relationship with strong emotional bonds and solid roots developed over the years can provide motivation and emotional support needed for success and security.

A solid relationship provides an emotional home base where you can express feelings and develop a support system that allows you to handle adversity. You can be yourself and take refuge from a world that is sometimes hostile and unsympathetic. Having this kind of security lowers stress and increases self-esteem.

Unfortunately, many relationships lack this level of intimacy. Some couples are more like roommates who have sex and share a common living space. In this type of arrangement, work and leisure activities are top priorities, which often leads to depression, anxiety, lack of direction, and decreased emotional energy.

When things are balanced, work provides the financial means to achieve relationship goals, and leisure activities are outlets for recharging energy and providing fun. But your top goal, short-term and long-term, is making your partner a friend, lover, and soulmate. Your partner is never a second choice.

80. *How can I nurture our relationship?*

Nurturing—putting in the kind of extra effort you devote to career, hobbies, children, and other commitments—means creating a warm, secure environment in which the partnership can flourish. Both of you must give conscious attention to staying close, trusting, and loving.

Many of the problems couples face today stem from a reluctance to focus attention on the partnership. People feel unappreciated, frustrated, bored, and depressed; both partners think there is something missing.

To nurture your partner, make him your number-one priority. Support his growth and sincerely care about his feelings and needs. (Of course, this must be reciprocal; a lopsided arrangement leads only to resentment, bitterness, and alienation.)

Nurturing can be as simple as kissing your partner hello and voicing appreciation. Show love and generosity of spirit. How about helping your partner with his yard work? Or cleaning the kitchen after dinner so your mate can relax?

Nothing, though, is more nurturing than unconditional acceptance. Knowing that he has his best friend waiting at the end of a long day is one of the most gratifying thoughts your partner can have.

81. Are public displays of affection really acceptable?

Affection is a sweet common denominator of love. When you give your partner a hug or kiss, you strengthen bonds of love. Displays of affection carry splendid messages; these are signs that you love and cherish your partner. Touching affectionately in public is a joyful way to raise the level of loving feelings.

Of course, some people keep feelings hidden (many were raised in families who downplayed displays of emotion). But intimacy-building calls for breaking through barriers. Stretch yourself and find ways to open up and lose old inhibitions about sharing affection, verbally and physically.

If your partner avoids expressing affection, help him work to break down barriers, and he may learn to share public embraces, kisses, and other signs of love.

82. Does body language reveal desire?

She is playing with her hair. He is gesturing wildly, moving toward her as he speaks. Yes, indeed, body language shows warm, positive feelings—

as well as negative ones. In the early stages of a relationship, body language is used to flirt. Eye contact and body positions show the level of attention and convey attraction.

When you are sitting in a restaurant, watch a couple's body language and you will be able to tell how well they like each other. Look for small, loving gestures; full, undivided attention; and cozy closeness, all of which reveal intimacy.

In fact, the same body language you used in courting can convey intimate feelings throughout your relationship. Nonetheless, most of us have no idea what kind of messages we are sending. But you can learn to make your signals count. To show interest, nod your head during conversation, make eye contact, face your partner, and give him your undivided attention. (If you glance away, avoid eye contact, or turn your body away, you are sending the message that you really are not interested.)

If your relationship is warm and loving, messages should be consistent with those feelings. Being attentive, smiling, open, and responsive will reinforce your loving verbal expressions.

83. How far should I go to please my mate?

Sharing, openness, and good communication build the trust that supports connectedness. Wanting to please is wonderful and appropriate, but you should never compromise yourself, your integrity, or your self-respect.

With intimate partners, natural give and take exists. Problems arise only when one partner feels inadequate or unloved and tries desperately to satisfy the other to an unhealthy degree. Usually, that partner feels unworthy of receiving love. He may feel criticized and powerless. This fuels inequality that bars intimacy.

You and your partner should try to build an unconditionally accepting relationship in which love can grow effortlessly. Relationships that are egalitarian have mutual respect and acceptance. Partners please without struggling because they are confident and trusting. They praise each other and behave in ways that nurture the partnership.

84. Is a positive, optimistic attitude a must for strong intimacy?

If you think positively, you will not get stuck in setbacks. This keeps your mood upbeat and allows you to deal with frustrations.

Successful couples always look forward with hope. In general, optimistic people are simply healthier, more creative, and better adjusted. Optimists know they will come out on top, and they do. Life is full of challenges that they accept and conquer.

In short, positive attitudes can determine to a large extent the success of the relationship. People with unhappy, pessimistic thoughts breed negative, defeatist attitudes. Partners who fail to persevere through tough times have trouble meeting goals, and it is not uncommon for them to experience depression. Such people have more marital conflict than other couples since their relationship goals tend to be fragmented from prior failures.

It is important in a successful intimate relationship to have goals, but the only way to meet them is through staying positive during difficulties. This enables you to build on prior successes.

Partners who succeed have stronger bonds. The overall slant of the partnership is successful, and both partners are undaunted by challenges.

If your partnership lacks a positive tilt, reassess your goals and your focus. Setting realistic goals will help. Work to think positive—always—and respond with optimism. If your partner is pessimistic, make changes that will lead to a can-do attitude. This will create a more intimate relationship because you'll be a successful loving team.

85. How can I avoid taking my partner for granted?

You fell in love for many reasons. Unique qualities attracted you and made you fall in love. Continue to take note of those qualities and comment on them to your partner, friends, and family. This helps to keep these special qualities fresh in your mind and your partner's. Compliments are nourishment.

If you take your partner—or your relationship—for granted, your life together will become tedious, boring, and passionless. In the hustle and bustle of everyday life, it is easy to forget the many things your partner does for you, but remembering to praise one another for routine tasks is important to making him feel appreciated. Gifts can also lift the heart and make your partner feel special, and you don't have to wait for special occasions. Give unnecessary, fun, touching gifts that communicate love. Be silly, inventive, and generous. What you give does not have to be expensive. It can be a gift of time (sleeping late, taking a bubble bath undisturbed, going out to do something fun without having to worry about everyday chores). These can be some of the best presents in our hurried, time-pressed lives.

What is important is that you give with a heart full of love. Show awareness of your partner's needs. Notice what is going on in his life, and reaffirm your connection and your love.

86. How can I show my loyalty and devotion?

Loyalty and devotion deepen love. You find that it is all right to feel vulnerable and needy. You do not experience emotional insecurity because both of you give and receive love.

Attraction and chemistry bring a couple together; common goals and interests hold them together; but commitment and trust through expressions of loyalty and devotion make the partnership solidly bonded. The ability to express passion and release inhibitions and fears increases when partners truly trust. Knowing that someone is there for you forever gives you the support needed to discover the fires of sexual passion and the deepest levels of intimacy within the soul. An intimate relationship is a source of joy only if you have faith in your partner's loyalty, devotion, and enduring dependability.

87. How can I show that I appreciate my partner?

Ask yourself this: If someone asked your partner whether you appreciated him, what would he say? Would the answer be a quick "yes," or would he have to think about it for a while?

One of the ways to keep a relationship fresh is showing appreciation for your partner. Let him know you adore and admire him, and you will be fanning the flames of love. For intimacy to grow, you must thank your mate for being there for you; tell him you're glad he wants you; and let him know you treasure and honor the relationship daily.

If you are not quite sure how you have been treating your partner, you can be sure that you are edging close to the trap of indifference. Couples fall into negative patterns easily: they become callous to each other's feelings; they act bossy; they take each other for granted. But you can sidestep these problems by showing appreciation, in actions and words.

Every day of your life, acknowledge and respect the person you love. No matter how long you have been together, no matter how much you expect certain behavior, remember that thriving love requires effort and gracious acknowledgment of each other.

You must hold your beloved in high regard, and treat him as a person deserving of respect, kindness, and appreciation. This gives depth to a partnership and stirs the sparks of interest, desire, and passion.

88. *What is the secret to keeping the sensual aspect of our relationship intact?*

In movies, we see couples who drool over each other. They are madly in love, wildly passionate. And most of us can remember the early days of a relationship, when we were similarly brainless and smitten. So, how can a loving pair sustain sensuality?

No one needs to tell us that relationships can become dull, lifeless, and drained without the inspiration provided by sensuality. It is easy for couples to become preoccupied with nonsexual aspects of life that make it tense.

So, why not let sensuality serve as a source of arousal and diversion? Get in touch with your sensual side by becoming attuned to mind- and muscle-relaxing stimuli. Tap your senses for arousing and relaxing effects.

Delight your partner's body with fingers, hands, feathers, silk scarves, hot towels, flower petals, and heated oils. Shampoo his hair or lather his body in a bath or shower. Enjoy the feel of your fingers in his hair, the smell of shampoo, the shape of his body as you gently massage. Enjoy touching and being touched, and take your time.

Another sensual activity: Ask your partner to lie down and close his eyes; then have him try to identify objects with different tastes and textures, such as ice cubes, whipped cream, chocolate, feathers, silk. The options are endless. Blindfold your mate and feed him strawberries or ice cream, as a perfect lead-in to sensual fun.

Combine sensual massage with tasting. Add romantic music and scented candles. Make sensual aromas part of every erotic experience.

When you explore, satisfy, and pleasure your partner in new ways, you experience togetherness in a passionate, playful manner, which is wonderful for developing intimacy.

89. *How can we keep our relationship joyful and fun?*

How long has it been since you acted childlike and lighthearted? If it has been more than a week, that is too long. Every day or so, you need to delight in play—cast off obligations and responsibilities for a time and rekindle the child within you.

Let yourself revert to a time when life was new and full of excitement. Play as much as you can and unleash that wonderful carefree spirit.

Most couples get so caught up in being grownups, with tons of responsibilities, that they forget how to let loose and play. But if you allow yourself to view life as nothing but chores and grimness, you will lose your zest and youthful vigor. Along to road to maturity, many people completely forget how to enjoy life.

Having fun keeps you functioning at an optimal level, and what better recreation than playing with a partner you love? Look for ways to have carefree experiences and abandon seriousness. Even shared silliness can deepen bonds. Seeing your mate at his most innocent and unguarded will help you appreciate the lovable child within and remind you of the qualities that make him precious to you.

- Try a new game.
- Figure out what your spouse loves to do.
- Take walks together (hold hands if you are slow-walkers).
- Do something together for other people less fortunate: volunteer for a soup kitchen, gather canned goods for the homeless, read to people at a seniors' home.
- Tickle his back in bed at night—and hope that he will reciprocate. It is a sweet, touchy thing that makes you feel loved and nurtured.
- Share insider jokes, movies, sayings.
- Each morning, seize the day and share your joy with your spouse. (If he is a quiet guy who wakes up slowly, don't whistle!)

Love flourishes between partners who can balance home, work, children, play, and intimacy. Keep in mind that sexual intimacy is a form of play; let yourself go—have fun and laugh and love.

90. What is the best way to avoid falling into a rut?

Keeping a little bit of mystique about you will go a long way toward keeping your mate on his toes and interested in you. Do whatever you can to avoid monotony, which makes a relationship dull and predictable. If you are having sex in the same place, at the same time, with the same approach, work on becoming more adventuresome. Do something daring or unconventional so that you will not lose that magical connection that first brought you together.

In the beginning of a relationship, partners make a point of planning opportunities to experience erotic pleasure or do exciting things as a couple. Simply continuing those actions can help your partnership stay interesting.

Some common joy-stealers are: workaholism, money complaints, life-is-grim attitudes. Why not look at these things and talk about how destructive they are to your happiness? No matter what your age, it is never too late to start doing better. Revel in life; do not get bogged down in the mundane, nitty-gritty stuff.

One of your top priorities should be making time for things that can make your relationship intimate and fun. It takes creativity, time, and energy to keep passion and friendship alive.

91. Is it important for us to spend our leisure time together?

The happiest couples share a great deal of leisure time. Shared time in fun activities keeps the friendship vibrant. Couples who enjoy each other usually want to spend time together; they create opportunities because they love each other's company.

So, why do most couples spend very little leisure time together? Often, it is because of work schedules, different biological clocks, family obligations, and a lack of common interests. But, why not explore activities you can share? For true intimacy, schedule joint fun. If one of you is a night person and the other's a morning person, find times when you are both energetic. And make the most of periods when you are away from work and kids. (Be sure to express your appreciation when your partner frees up time to be with you.)

To be great friends and happy partners, you must spend fun leisure time together. If you do not do that, intimacy will wane.

92. How can I show pride in my partner's achievements?

Sharing your partner's successes creates a spirit of togetherness that fosters intimacy. Applauding your partner's accomplishments makes both of you feel successful. Support his dreams and aspirations, and cheer him on in everything he does.

One thing is a given. Your mate will always remember your support—or lack of it. Even if you are frustrated because your partner's project takes him away from you at times, a failure to show support is a mistake because your resentment weakens team spirit. Nor should you point out flaws in your partner's aspirations, as if you are telling him "I know better." Your partner wants a mate, not a parent. Communicate your concerns in other ways.

By encouraging your mate to pursue his goals, you become part of the inspiration. Respond enthusiastically when your partner involves you in his plans. Everyone has dreams of glory, and your involvement solidifies bonds of togetherness. You provide support because you are intimate partners. Giving less would be unthinkable.

93. *What is the best way to console my partner when he is feeling down?*

You are in a great position to be the healer of his heart during painful times. When overwhelmed by sorrow or stress, he needs your presence, reassurance, strength, and love. If he is hurting emotionally, he needs your comforting embrace.

When tragedy strikes, your partner may first pull away and become distant, but you should still offer affection, solace, and understanding. Step into his sorrow to comfort with your presence, ability to listen, supportive words, and loving touch. Make sure he knows that he is not alone. When your partner feels like his loss is unbearable, your consolation can bolster his spirits. Give love that's unconditional, regardless of how his loss affects you. By the same token, your partner can help you through difficult times better than anyone else. Be supportive and you will be cherished.

94. *Are small reassurances important?*

Sometimes, the smallest reassurances have the biggest impact. When in doubt, do not hesitate to do things that show your love. The more you give, the more you receive. Everyone needs constant reassurance. Never fall into the trap of being stingy with love because you fear that you will not get the love you need.

Shower your mate with kisses, hugs, kindness, compliments, letters, cards, literary creations, celebrations, passion, praise, gifts, and love. Be inventive, creative, and mysterious. Make your gestures fun and memorable.

Expressing love in small ways shows your partner that you cherish him. Lift the level of your relationship from ordinary to extraordinary by capturing your mate's attention and heart with frequent reminders of love. If you want your mate to feel adored, never underestimate the power of a small gesture, a kind word, or a loving surprise. Giving someone a morsel of your time is a big gift.

VII

Control/Criticism

95. How destructive are power struggles?

Power struggles. Who rules the roost? Or should this question even come up—in view of the fact that coupledom is supposed to call for a partnership mentality. When you think you are being controlled, you will resist your partner's initiatives, either overtly or in a passive-aggressive manner. You become combatants rather than allies. Soon, you lose respect for each other, and a void in decision-making authority appears. Worried that team survival depends on you alone, you may try to outdo your partner, leading to a battle of wills. If you lay down the law without inviting input, resentment results. And when both of you struggle for authority, conflict is inevitable, and you waste a great deal of unproductive energy. Romance and lovemaking fall by the wayside when you are concentrating on getting your way. One partner feels victorious; the other feels defeated. Clearly, in war, there is no intimacy.

When winning becomes more important than finding common ground, take steps to avoid power struggles. Try to hear and respect your partner's point of view without defending yourself. Seek to establish true sharing of decision-making. A spirit of teamwork will lead to mutual sharing of power.

96. *Will constructive criticism ruin our relationship?*

Criticism. Even the word has a bad ring to it. Your partner may cringe when he gets a feeling that you are about to go in this direction. Which is your approach? Do you offer your perceptions to improve a situation—or do you criticize in a derogatory manner that hurts and belittles?

Offered incorrectly, even criticism that is warranted will be hurtful. Further, in a close relationship, improper criticism destroys intimacy over time.

When you criticize hurtfully, it puts your mate on the defensive. Feeling defensive, he probably won't hear what you want nor will he respond in a positive way. Typically, someone attacked will withdraw or defend with a counter attack. The result? Your partner feels inadequate, overwhelmed, degraded.

If you are the critic, does your need to speak out stem from insecurity, resentment, jealousy, or irrational thinking? If your goal is to control, minimize, or hurt your partner, think twice before going that route. On the other hand, criticism offered graciously can serve as encouragement. Try the following:

- Welcome criticism that is given in a respectful, concerned, and supportive manner.
- View criticism positively. It can simply be an invitation to change for the better.
- Before offering words of criticism, make your partner feel secure. If you often praise your partner, words of criticism will be seen in a positive light.
- Never confront, attack, or accuse.
- Ask for explanations. Ask for opinions.

• Ask your partner to consider alternatives. Do this by asking questions that underscore weaknesses in your partner's views. This gentle approach will open your partner's mind to other options. A respectful approach increases the chances of having your criticism heard. Along the way, you may discover that your behavior needs some work, too.

97. What is the best way to avoid being rigid?

Is your partner a my-way-or-the-highway kind of mate? If so, it is important to sway him to the merits of collaboration. Trust and mutual respect go hand and hand with intimacy.

If you think that your partner is rigid, suggest adjustments to involve both of you actively in decision-making. Seek your partner's input, and listen when he gives it—then offer your thoughts. Good listening skills and a willingness to appreciate your mate's thoughts are important. The best solutions come from collaboration.

How can you recognize a couple whose flexibility works? They laugh and talk easily. They accept new situations. They alter their perceptions with a flexible approach. Compromise is a concept they work on year-round.

98. How can we keep from placing blame during arguments?

Gimme a scapegoat. Some people truly love tracking down the culprits behind dirty deeds. Placing blame is a habit that goes far back into childhood days, when we sought to escape punishment by making sure our parents and teachers knew who the real villains were. Not us!

But adults should have moved beyond childish, unproductive behavior, and blaming is a perfect example because it is extremely destructive. Accusing your partner of being at fault places total responsibility on one person and underscores your own reluctance to admit wrongdoing.

Blaming also diminishes the other person because hurtful attacks demoralize and lead to anger, frustration, and anxiety. As a couple, you bicker rather than problem-solve.

If you have a tendency to blame your partner, try doing things differently.

- To avoid blaming, slow down your response. Think before you speak when something has taken place that bothers you.
- Reflect on the meaning and outcome of your words.
- Assess the situation. Ask yourself and your partner questions about what has taken place.
- Readily accept responsibility if you are at fault. At first, it will feel strange, but soon you'll feel good about doing it.
- Remember that intimacy requires the ability to resolve conflict smoothly.

99. How should I handle my partner's need to control me?

Someone has to be in charge here! That is the lament of those marriage partners sometimes known as battle-axes, overbearing husbands, ball-breakers—the list goes on and on.

But all of us fall into this pattern at one time or another. To get your partner to do what you want him to, you exert influence in a way that's manipulative or too forceful. This insensitive behavior may work, but it also builds resentment.

This is often the approach of men who were raised to think that they should dominate in relationships. For them, letting a woman have equal say is not macho. Attempts to dominate, taken to extreme, can result in physical and mental abuse. By the same token, many women grow up learning to take a passive role in a relationship, which invites domination. Under stress, partners often revert to culturally taught roles.

On the other hand, some couples like to have one person controlling the relationships. A woman may prefer to let her man take charge, and the man likes this role and doesn't abuse it.

But problems arise when partners are engaged in a power struggle—when one fails to see the benefits of democratic roles. Resentment and anger rule, and such relationships rarely succeed. Interestingly, some couples briefly have better sex under this type of duress, but ultimately, sexual escapes fail. Most people do not want to be locked in a domination struggle. Even passive partners who accept being subservient dislike having their self-esteem trampled on, and, eventually, they hate being manipulated.

Some people let a partner dominate just to keep the peace and maintain the relationship. However, failure to speak up is stifling, and it is important to say what you think. If you are passive and your partner is assertive, you must be heard when you do express yourself—or you will wind up feeling manipulated.

Your partner must value your opinions, no matter who is making a decision. And you must believe he cares what you think.

100. How can I learn to be less demanding?

A good rule of thumb: Don't speak to your mate in a way that is less respectful than you would treat a close friend. (You would never yell at a buddy to get his elbows off the table, would you?) Communicate with patience, tolerance, and love, and pay close attention to your words and the tone of your voice.

Over time, the way you talk to your spouse may have changed. Those sweet endearments and soft words may have been replaced with quicker, louder speech. No longer do you hear (or offer) the loving tone you used during courtship. You may sound impatient, as if you are rushing to issue demands without taking time to explain or listen. You may even have moved into war-zone lingo, with maneuvers and retaliation—verbal attacks that reflect hostility.

When you realize that you've gotten into a habit of communicating without respect, point it out and make a conscious effort to improve. Practice speaking more softly and slowly. Use relaxed, open body language. Make good eye contact.

The way you talk to each other has a huge effect on your closeness. Good communication helps you avoid bickering, and you are less likely to misinterpret messages. Partners who are equals respect each other's feelings.

These tips will help you stay on target:

- Always consider the effect your words will have on your partner.
- Bear in mind that helpful advice in a harsh tone of voice comes across as criticism.

Remember that intimate relationships are based on loving, respectful, thoughtful communication.

About the Authors

Marvin Stone, M.D. is a graduate of New York Medical College and completed his residency in psychiatry at Bellevue Hospital in New York City. Dr. Stone has been practicing general psychiatry, marital therapy and sex therapy for over twenty years and is a fellow of the American Psychiatric Association. Dr. Stone resides in Houston, Texas.

Cari La Grange Murphy is an accomplished freelance writer specializing in the fields of psychology, spirituality, health/fitness and relationships. She has completed her second book entitled *Your Soul is Calling You* and she resides in Houston, Texas where she is working on her third book.

Diane Stafford has been a key figure in a number of magazines including *Houston Home and Garden* (editor-in-chief), *Houston Health and Fitness* (Founder/Editor-in-chief), *Latin Music Magazine* (Senior Editor), *Philanthropy in Texas* (editor) and *Texas Woman Magazine* (founder and editor-in-chief). Stafford now works as a free lance writer and edits books for Arte Publico Press.

www.ingramcontent.com/pod-product-compliance
Lightning Source LLC
Chambersburg PA
CBHW031231280526
45784CB00004B/1523